simple ways to success

indian

Das Sreedharan

photography by Peter Cassidy

This edition first published in 2003 by Quadrille Publishing Limited
Alhambra House, 27-31 Charing Cross Road, London WC2H OLS

Editorial director Jane O'Shea **Creative director** Helen Lewis
Managing editor Janet Illsley **Art director** Vanessa Courtier **Editor** Jenni Muir
Photographer Peter Cassidy **Food stylist** Sunil Vijayakar **Props stylist** Jane Campsie
Copy editor Kathy Steer **Designer** Sue Storey **Production** Vincent Smith and Beverley Richardson

Text © 2003 Das Sreedharan Photography © 2003 Pete Cassidy
Design and layout © 2003 Quadrille Publishing Limited

Cataloguing in Publication Data: a catalogue record for this book is available from the British Library.

ISBN 1 84400 069 9
Printed in China

contents

NOTES

All spoon measures are level unless otherwise stated:
1 teaspoon = 5 ml spoon; 1 tablespoon = 15 ml spoon.

Use fresh herbs unless dried herbs are suggested.

Use freshly ground black pepper unless otherwise stated.

Free-range eggs are recommended and large eggs should be used
except where a different size is specified.

Recipes which feature raw or lightly cooked eggs should be avoided
by anyone who is pregnant or in a vulnerable health group.

introduction

Although British people love to eat Indian food, many have been put off cooking it at home because they believe the dishes are too complicated and require a lot of strange ingredients. To me, this is a sad misperception. Throughout India there are many wonderful examples of simple home cooking using ingredients readily available on supermarket shelves in this country. And there is nothing I would like better than to tell you more about these recipes.

Since moving to England and establishing my first restaurant, it has been my mission to promote the kind of food I was fortunate enough to enjoy while growing up in Kerala, South India's largest state. Like most people, I still think my mother is the best cook in the world! Many of the dishes I prepare today – whether in the restaurants, during my cookery evenings for customers, or at home with my wife Alison – are those I adored when I was young. Like many Asians, our family was vegetarian and daily meals were healthy combinations of fresh vegetables, fruits, yogurt and nuts, with many of the ingredients grown in our own garden.

Over the years I have also collected many recipes from friends and colleagues while travelling throughout India. The ones I have chosen for this book come from various communities with substantially different religious and cultural traditions. Like the South Indian recipes (which are themselves from a lively cultural mix), they use ingredients that are easy to find and methods that are simple and quick. There are meat dishes including Goan pork vindaloo and Kashmiri lamb rojan josh, chicken and vegetable dishes from Bengal, and many recipes using the dairy products and pulses beloved throughout North India.

In addition, I am including several of our restaurants' most popular dishes and new creations developed during my cookery evenings. I really enjoy taking ingredients such as courgette and cauliflower, which I never knew as a child, and creating new Indian dishes from them. Fusing Northern and Southern Indian cooking styles is also a great passion, but that doesn't mean the resulting dishes are complicated – some of them contain as few as six ingredients.

A few Indian techniques, such as making spice blends, may seem a little daunting at first, but you will be astonished at how quick and easy they are. The blender you already use to whiz soups until smooth works equally well as a grinder for producing fragrant pastes, sauces and batters. Soon you will be doing so with confidence, as well as quickly grating fresh coconut in the food processor, and softening tamarind pulp to add a sour fruity flavour to curries.

My mother always said that no one can teach you to cook. She said: 'I will show you how I do it, but you have to learn to do it your way.' This is an important tradition in India. You should feel free to adapt the quantities of spices, oil, water and main ingredients given in these recipes to suit your own taste. I do hope that you enjoy using this book and that it inspires you to cook more often. It doesn't matter whether the food you prepare is South Indian, North Indian, or Italian, I honestly believe that home cooking is the foundation of good health and happiness.

ingredients

You won't need an extensive array of spices and authentic flavourings to prepare my recipes, but here is a guide to the special ingredients that feature in this book.

Banana leaves

Elongated banana leaves are used in South India and other tropical Asian countries to wrap foods for cooking, such as fish for steaming, in much the same way as aluminium foil is used in the West. They can also take the place of serving plates.

To use banana leaves in cooking, first soften by holding over a flame or dipping in a dish of warm water for 30 seconds. This will make the leaves pliable and easy to fold.

Chana dal

These robust yellow lentils are derived from a brown variety of pea that is skinned and split. They look very similar to yellow split lentils and have a sweet and nutty aroma. Chana dal is combined with meat in curries, ground with lamb to make a paste for kebabs, and frequently cooked with vegetables, especially squashes. In Kerala it is used to make sweet as well as savoury dishes.

Chillies

The wide range of chillies available today can be confusing, but in Keralan dishes and for the recipes featured in this book, there are only two types that you need to buy. Small dried red chillies, 2.5–3cm (1–1½ inches) long, are available from the spice rack, and fresh green chillies, about 7.5cm (3 inches) long, are sold in the fresh produce department.

Chillies are renowned for the fiery heat they bring to dishes, and this makes some people wary of them. However, their heat can be controlled. You can bring chilli flavour to a recipe without strong heat by using the chilli whole rather than slicing or chopping it. To do this, make just one cut about two-thirds of the way along the length of the chilli to release the flavour before adding it to the pan. Where chillies are sliced or chopped, I rarely deseed them but you may prefer to do so for a milder flavour.

Coconut

The large hairy brown coconut is indigenous to several areas, one of which is South India, and the freshly grated white flesh of the nut is essential to Keralan cooking. It is used in an amazing variety of ways, including vegetable side dishes, breads, curries, savoury snacks and sweet dishes, and appears in some form at every meal.

Unsweetened desiccated coconut can often be used in place of freshly grated coconut in dishes, but it has a much drier texture and the result is not as succulent. It is far better to use the fresh nut.

To extract the flesh from a fresh coconut, insert a metal skewer in the eye of the coconut and drain the water into a jug. Using a heavy tool, such as a butcher's steel or cleaver, carefully crack the shell around the middle and separate the inner nut from the hairy casing. You can then use a vegetable peeler to make long shavings of coconut flesh, or an ordinary kitchen grater to grate it. When only a small amount is required, a citrus zester will give you fine shreds quickly and easily. To prepare a substantial quantity of fresh coconut, place the pieces of coconut flesh in a food processor and process until finely chopped.

Coconut milk

Do not confuse this with the clear water inside a fresh coconut. Coconut milk is a manufactured product, made by pouring hot water over grated coconut flesh, then pushing through a sieve to give a thin white liquid. Coconut cream is similar, but has a much thicker consistency. Coconut milk is used as the base for many South Indian dishes and is readily available in cans and long-life packs.

Curry leaves

Curry leaves come from a plant with the botanical name of *Murraya koenigi* and are thought to smell and taste like curry powder. While the taste is spicy, it is also nutty, a quality brought out when the curry leaves are lightly fried in oil until just crisp. They are used as herbs in cooking, most often added whole, but sometimes chopped first. Bay leaves may look similar, but they have a very different flavour and are not an appropriate substitute. Don't hesitate to buy a substantial bunch of curry leaves when you see them on sale. For convenience, they can be stored in the freezer wrapped in foil or sealed in a polythene bag, and added to dishes as and when required.

Ghee

Highly popular in North India, ghee is the Indian version of clarified butter. That is butter which has had all its milk solids removed. The process involves melting the butter over a low heat, then simmering it until all the moisture has evaporated and the milk solids have separated from the fat. The milk solids are then removed to leave a pure fat, which is excellent for frying at high temperatures. It also has a long shelf life – so much so that ghee is sold in cans on the supermarket shelf rather than in the fresh dairy section.

Jaggery and palm sugar

An unrefined form of sugar, jaggery is dark, sticky and crumbly. Made from the juice of crushed sugar cane, it is less sweet than ordinary white or brown sugars and has an extraordinary musky flavour. Palm sugar from countries such as Thailand has a comparable rich, complex taste and is a reasonable substitute for Indian jaggery in cooking. Brown and demerara sugars lack this earthy quality, but the recipes in this book will work if you use them.

Paneer

India's best-known cheese is often described as a 'cottage' or 'curd' cheese because it is usually freshly made in the home. However, paneer is drained and pressed, which makes it very different from the cottage and curd cheese known in Britain. Paneer's firmer texture means it can be cut into cubes, then fried or grilled until golden while still retaining its square shape. Look for it in the chiller cabinets alongside other cooking cheeses.

Plantains

Sometimes referred to as cooking bananas, plantains look rather like large bananas, but have a thicker green skin and starchier, less sweet flesh. This fruit plays an important role in South Indian cooking and several different varieties grow in Kerala alone. When green, or unripe, they are used as a vegetable in curries, and when ripe they are steamed and eaten for breakfast.

Rice

Fragrant basmati rice is often regarded as the supreme Asian rice variety, but we tend not to use it on a daily basis in India because it is expensive by comparison to other locally grown varieties. Basmati rice also has a unique aroma, which can be lost when combined with many strongly flavoured ingredients. The recipes in this book indicate when regular long grain white rice is appropriate.

Rice flour

Fine, white, powdery rice flour is commonly used for batters and doughs in South India, and to make soft rice noodle cakes. It can also be used as a thickening agent, in the same way as cornflour. Rice flour has a mild flavour that is delicately sweet, but not so much that it detracts from savoury dishes.

Spices

My home state of Kerala is known as the 'spice box' of India but I have limited the range of spices in this book, so you won't have to buy more than you are comfortable with. Spices that feature most often in my cooking include whole brown mustard seeds, ground turmeric, cumin, coriander and cinnamon. Using mustard seeds in the way I do doesn't impart a strong mustard flavour, but a slightly crunchy texture. Turmeric is India's most widely used spice and brings a mellow flavour and golden colour to dishes. Cumin is one of the most versatile spices. It can take on different flavours depending on how it is treated – used whole, ground, toasted, fried or raw. Garam masala, which means 'hot spices' is a convenient ready-made mix of ground spices, and is aromatic rather than fiery. Almost every Indian kitchen has its favourite blend, but most contain black peppercorns, cardamom, cinnamon, cumin, cloves and mace.

Tamarind pulp

This tart fruit is used in South Indian and Gujarati cooking as a souring agent and brings a tangy contrast to mild coconut sauces. It is also used for chutneys and drinks. Sold in dried blocks with a long shelf life, tamarind pulp needs to be soaked in hot water for about 20 minutes to soften the fruit, then pushed through a sieve to remove any seeds and fibres. The resulting liquid is stirred into dishes. Although the process of making tamarind liquid is always the same, recipes can vary in the intensity of liquid required, so the ratio of tamarind to hot water varies accordingly.

Urad dal

The small black lentils used to make urad dal are found in a variety of forms in India. In the North, the whole black lentils are favoured, while in Southern India (and in all of my recipes) the lentils are invariably skinned and split. Although these are also known as black gram dal, the term is confusing because South Indian urad dal is cream in colour. It is rather like a spice, added to dishes to provide a nutty flavour and crunchy texture.

Yogurt

Thick and creamy yogurt is made everyday in homes across the Indian subcontinent and is an important part of every meal, most commonly enjoyed plain as a mild contrast to spicy food. Raitas – cooling salads made with yogurt and crunchy vegetables – are very popular. Yogurt is also often churned into cooling drinks with spices, and is the base for many desserts. In savoury cooking, its main role is as a souring agent. Any thick creamy plain yogurt will work for the recipes in this book but avoid any brands that are very sharp and acidic in flavour.

1 starters, snacks and chutneys

mushroom and coconut uthappams

These rice pancakes are South India's answer to pizza. You can use any seasonal crunchy vegetables and herbs for the topping and the result can be very colourful. Uthappams are traditionally eaten with coconut chutney (page 30) and sometimes an elaborate sour lentil dish called sambar, but as long as your toppings are interesting, they are perfectly delicious served plain. Fenugreek seeds enhance the batter, but they are pungent so remember a little goes a very long way.

MAKES 8
300g (11oz) long-grain rice
75g (3oz) urad dal
1/2 teaspoon fenugreek seeds
vegetable oil, for frying
sea salt

FOR THE TOPPING:
100g (3½oz) mushrooms, sliced
1 red onion, peeled and finely sliced or chopped
2 green chillies
2 tablespoons chopped coriander leaves or
  curry leaves
50g (2oz) freshly grated coconut

1 Place the rice in a large bowl and cover with cold water. Place the urad dal and fenugreek seeds in another bowl and add sufficient cold water to cover generously. Set both bowls aside and leave to soak for at least 8 hours or overnight.

2 Drain the rice and dal, keeping them separate. Place the rice in a blender and process slowly for 2–3 minutes, gradually adding 125 ml (4 fl oz) water to make a smooth paste. Transfer to a large bowl. Place the urad dal and fenugreek seeds in the rinsed-out blender and process slowly for 5 minutes, gradually adding 4 tablespoons water to make a batter. Add the dal mixture to the rice paste and mix well. Stir in a little salt and cover with a damp cloth. Set aside to ferment for 12 hours or overnight.

3 When ready to cook, the batter should have increased in volume and become a mass of small bubbles. Stir a little water into the batter to give a thick pouring consistency. Heat a griddle or large, heavy-based frying pan until very hot, then lightly brush with oil. Assemble the topping ingredients and divide into 8 portions.

4 Pour a ladleful of the batter on to the griddle and spread it out slightly with the back of a spoon until about 10cm (4 inches) in diameter, about the size and thickness of an English pancake. Top with a portion of the mushrooms, onion, chilli and coriander or curry leaves, pressing them gently into the batter, then sprinkle lightly with the coconut. Cook for 2 minutes or until the bottom is golden brown.

5 Brush the edges of the uthappam with oil and carefully turn it over with a spatula. Cook on the other side for 2–3 minutes until the batter is cooked and the onion and mushrooms have browned slightly. Remove and keep warm while you cook the remaining uthappams. Serve with coconut chutney (page 30) or as a bread-like accompaniment to 'wet' curries.

lentil and spinach vadai

'Vadai! Vadai! Vadai!' is the typical hawker cry heard in most railway stations in India. These crunchy, coarsely ground lentil patties are also very popular afternoon snacks in teashops. They have an amazing flavour and can be made with various lentils, but this version featuring chana dal is one of my favourites. If you are unable to find chana dal, substitute yellow split peas.

SERVES 4

400g (14oz) chana dal, or yellow split peas
200g (7oz) spinach leaves, tough stalks removed
1 onion, peeled and finely chopped
2 green chillies, finely sliced or chopped

2.5cm (1 inch) piece fresh root ginger, peeled and finely chopped
10 curry leaves, finely chopped
vegetable oil, for deep-frying
sea salt

1 Place the chana dal in a large bowl, cover with water and set aside to soak for 1 hour. Meanwhile, place the spinach in a large saucepan over a low heat with just the water clinging to the leaves after washing and cook, stirring occasionally, for 1 minute or until just wilted. Set aside to cool, then chop finely. Tip the soaked dal into a sieve and drain thoroughly.

2 Transfer the dal to a blender and process for 2–3 minutes to a coarse paste – don't grind it too finely as you want some of the dal to remain whole to give the vadai a good texture. Tip into a large bowl and add the chopped spinach, onion, chillies, ginger, curry leaves and a little salt. Mix thoroughly to make a thick paste.

3 Divide the mixture into portions, about the size of a golf ball, then roll each one between your palms and gently flatten into a small round patty. The mixture will make about 20 patties.

4 Heat the oil in a deep-fryer, wok or large, heavy-based saucepan to 180–190°C or until a cube of bread browns in 30 seconds. Deep-fry the patties in batches for 5 minutes or until deep golden. Remove with a slotted spoon and drain on kitchen paper. Serve hot or cold.

onion bhajis

This is the simplest and cheapest snack you can make – no wonder it features on every Indian restaurant menu. To be honest, I wasn't keen on onion bhajis when I lived in India, but I became interested in them when I moved to London and Muslim friends would make them for the Ramadan fast. Bhajis can be made with various vegetables, including greens, so don't hesitate to experiment with the basic recipe.

Illustrated on previous page

SERVES 4

2 onions, peeled and finely sliced
175g (6oz) chick pea flour
50g (2oz) coriander leaves, finely chopped
1cm (1/2 inch) piece fresh root ginger, peeled
  and finely chopped
1/2 teaspoon chilli powder
1/2 teaspoon ground turmeric
pinch of crushed coriander seeds
vegetable oil, for deep-frying
sea salt

1 In a large bowl, mix together the onion slices, chick pea flour, coriander leaves, ginger, chilli powder, turmeric, crushed coriander seeds and a little salt. Gradually mix in 500ml (16fl oz) water to make a thick batter.

2 Heat the oil in a deep-fryer, wok or large, heavy-based saucepan to 180–190°C or until a cube of bread browns in 30 seconds. Using a metal spoon, take a small portion of batter and shape roughly into a ball, then carefully drop into the hot oil and deep-fry for 3–4 minutes or until the bhaji is cooked through and has a crunchy, golden exterior. Cook the bhajis in batches of two or three, adding them to the oil one at a time. Remove with a slotted spoon and drain on kitchen paper. Serve hot.

bonda

The restaurants of Udupi in Karnataka are renowned for their bonda. These are incredibly tasty, filling snacks, made with potatoes and subtly flavoured with fresh ginger, curry leaves and sometimes cashew nuts. Here bonda are made special and more substantial by adding flavoursome ingredients such as chillies, onions and coriander. Tiny versions make great cocktail snacks. Serve with coconut chutney (page 30), sweet mango chutney (page 31), or with garlic and chilli pickle (page 27).

SERVES 4

400g (14oz) potatoes, peeled and cubed
4 tablespoons vegetable oil
1 teaspoon mustard seeds
1 teaspoon urad dal
20 curry leaves
2.5cm (1 inch) piece fresh root ginger, peeled and grated

2 onions, peeled and finely chopped
2 green chillies, finely sliced
1 teaspoon ground turmeric, plus extra to season
4 tablespoons finely chopped coriander leaves
125g (4oz) chick pea flour
vegetable oil, for deep-frying
sea salt

1   Cook the potatoes in a saucepan of lightly salted water for about 15 minutes until tender, then drain and mash. Set aside.

2   Heat the 4 tablespoons oil in a large frying pan. Add the mustard seeds and urad dal and cook, stirring constantly, for 1–2 minutes or until the dal turns brown. Add the curry leaves, ginger and onions and cook, stirring occasionally, for 5 minutes.

3   Add the chillies and turmeric and cook for a further minute before adding the mashed potatoes and chopped coriander leaves. Stir over a low heat for 1 minute to ensure that the ingredients are thoroughly mixed, then remove the frying pan from the heat and set aside to cool.

4   Place the chick pea flour, a pinch of turmeric and a pinch of salt in a large bowl, then gradually stir in 275ml (9fl oz) water to make a smooth batter. Whisk until thoroughly blended, then set aside for 5 minutes.

5   Divide the potato mixture into small balls about the size of a golf ball. Heat the oil in a deep-fryer, wok or large, heavy-based saucepan to 180–190°C or until a cube of bread browns in 30 seconds. Cook the bonda in batches. Dip the potato balls in the batter and carefully drop them into the hot oil one by one, making sure that the pan is not overcrowded. Deep-fry for 3–4 minutes or until golden, then remove with a slotted spoon and drain on kitchen paper. Serve hot.

steamed rice and vegetable dumplings

These savoury *kozhukatta* or rice flour dumplings can be eaten as a snack at any time of the day, with a chutney or pickle. Or serve with a drizzle of spiced oil, made by frying a few curry leaves, dried red chilli, mustard seeds, coriander seeds and a pinch of chilli powder in oil until sizzling.

MAKES 12

about 225g (8oz) rice flour

1 tablespoon vegetable oil, plus extra to brush

sea salt

FOR THE FILLING:

2 tablespoons vegetable oil

1 teaspoon mustard seeds

50g (2oz) onion, peeled and finely chopped

1 teaspoon ground coriander

1/2 teaspoon chilli powder

1/2 teaspoon ground turmeric

25g (1oz) tomatoes, chopped

40g (1 1/2oz) peas

1 teaspoon freshly ground black pepper, or to taste

1 Put the rice flour and a little salt in a large bowl and make a well in the centre. Gradually stir in 175–250ml (6–8fl oz) warm water or just enough to make a smooth dough. Add the oil and mix to a soft dough, adding a little more flour or water if necessary.

2 For the filling, heat the oil in a large pan, add the mustard seeds and, as they start to pop, add the onion and a little salt. Cook for 5 minutes or until the onion is soft. Add the coriander, chilli powder and turmeric and mix well. Add the tomatoes and 4 tablespoons water and cook for 2 minutes. Stir in the peas and pepper, cover and simmer gently for 10–15 minutes until well cooked. Take off the heat.

3 Oil your hands, break off a piece of dough about the size of a golf ball and shape into a flat patty. Place a small spoonful of the filling in the middle of the patty and lightly fold the dough around it to enclose the filling. Gently roll into a ball and set aside on a plate. Repeat to use all the dough and filling.

4 Set a steamer over a large pan of water and bring to the boil. Put the dumplings in the steamer, cover and steam for 15 minutes or until the dough is cooked through. Serve hot or cold, allowing three each.

samosas

From humble beginnings in Punjabi homes and small *dhabas* (street cafés), samosas have become known the world over and were one of the first Indian foods to be sold ready-cooked in supermarkets. Making them at home with ready-made samosa pastry is easy, however, and allows greater flexibility with fillings. If samosa pastry isn't available, use filo instead. Each of the featured recipes is enough to fill 250g (9 oz) pastry, to serve 4.

Simply cut the samosa pastry into strips, 25 x 7.5cm (10 x 3 inches). Place 1 heaped tablespoon of filling in the middle at one end of a pastry strip. Fold a corner of the pastry over the mixture to form a triangle, then continue folding in alternate directions along the strip to make a triangular parcel.

Two-thirds fill a deep-fryer, heavy-based saucepan or wok with vegetable oil and heat to 180–190°C. Fry your samosas, one at a time, for 2–3 minutes until golden. Drain on kitchen paper, then serve hot or cold.

▲ green bean and pea filling
Heat 4 tbsp oil in a pan. Add 1 tsp mustard seeds and, when they start to pop, add 2 diced onions and fry until soft. Add 1 tsp ground coriander, 1 tsp chilli powder, ½ tsp garam masala, ½ tsp ground turmeric and a little salt. Fry for 1 minute, then add 2 diced potatoes, 1 diced carrot, 150g (5 oz) diced green beans and 150g (5 oz) peas. Cover and cook for 15 minutes. Remove from the heat and set aside to cool.

spicy potato filling

Boil 250g (9oz) cubed potatoes until tender; drain and mash lightly. Heat 4 tbsp oil in a frying pan and sauté 3 finely diced green chillies, 1 tsp shredded ginger and a pinch of cumin seeds for 1 minute. Add 1 finely diced onion and cook until soft. Add 1 tsp ground coriander, ½ tsp each garam masala and turmeric, and a little salt. Cook for 2 minutes, then stir in the potatoes and 4 tbsp chopped coriander leaves. Cool before using.

spiced lamb filling

Heat 5 tbsp oil in a pan and fry 3 chopped onions until soft and golden. Add 2 chopped tomatoes, 2 diced green chillies, 2 chopped garlic cloves, 1 tsp each chilli powder, garam masala and tomato purée, and a little salt; mix well. Add 250ml (8fl oz) water and bring to the boil. Stir in 100g (3½oz) cubed potatoes and 250g (9oz) lamb mince. Simmer, covered, for 20 minutes or until the mixture is well cooked and thick. Stir in 3 tbsp chopped coriander leaves and set aside to cool.

▲ vegetable and cashew nut filling

Boil 2 cubed potatoes in salted water for 5 minutes, add 50g (2oz) chopped cauliflower and cook for 2–3 minutes; drain. Heat 3 tbsp oil in a frying pan and fry 2 finely sliced onions, 2 diced green chillies and 75g (3oz) broken cashew nuts, for 4 minutes. Stir in ½ tsp each turmeric and garam masala. Add the potato mixture, 200g (7oz) finely sliced mushrooms and 50g (2oz) spinach. Cook, covered, for 4 minutes; the vegetables should be slightly crunchy. Stir in 4 tbsp chopped coriander leaves; cool.

beetroot cutlets

You may associate cutlets with lamb chops, but it is a different story in India where they are savoury cakes. The first time I ate beetroot cutlets was at a wedding engagement in a Christian friend's home, so I assumed it was a Christian speciality of our region. However, later in the week I had the same cutlet at Kumar's bakery in our town with a cup of tea. I then realised it was a new fashion in snack foods. The beetroot flavour was fascinating to me because I had only seen the vegetable used in curry dishes. Mr Kumar was kind enough to give me his recipe and I have subsequently made it many times.

MAKES 6

8 tablespoons vegetable oil
1 teaspoon mustard seeds
few curry leaves
2.5cm (1 inch) piece fresh root ginger, peeled and finely sliced
1 onion, peeled and finely sliced
1 teaspoon ground turmeric
1 teaspoon chilli powder
1 teaspoon garam masala
150g (5oz) cooked beetroot, peeled and finely diced
100g (3½oz) potatoes, finely diced
50g (2oz) peas
100ml (3½fl oz) milk
400g (14oz) breadcrumbs
sea salt

1 Heat 4 tablespoons oil in a large frying pan. Add the mustard seeds and, when they start to pop, add the curry leaves, ginger and onion. Fry for 5 minutes or until the onion is soft.

2 Stir in the turmeric, chilli powder and garam masala. Stir in the beetroot, potatoes and peas, then add about 100ml (3½fl oz) water and a little salt. Cook for 10 minutes or until the vegetables are very tender. Remove the pan from the heat and set aside to cool.

3 When the vegetable mixture is cool enough to handle, divide into 6 equal portions and form into teardrop-shaped cutlets.

4 Pour the milk into a shallow dish and spread the breadcrumbs out on a plate. Dip each beetroot cutlet into the milk, then into the breadcrumbs and turn to coat evenly, gently pressing the crumbs on to the cutlets to adhere.

5 Heat the remaining oil in a clean frying pan. You may need to cook the cutlets in two batches. Add them to the hot pan and fry for 3–5 minutes until crisp and golden, turning frequently. Drain on kitchen paper. Serve the cutlets hot, with kiwi fruit chutney (page 30) or date chutney (page 31).

garlic and chilli pickle

Garlic and chilli are common ingredients in Indian cooking, but combining the two to make pickle was chef Ramanathan's idea. He opened one of the first Indian restaurants in Britain and sadly passed away a few years ago, but the memory of his lovely pickle lingers on. It took me a while to discover how to make it, and even longer to make it close to his taste.

SERVES 8

4 tablespoons vegetable oil
pinch of fenugreek seeds
100g (3½oz) garlic cloves, peeled and sliced
1 teaspoon tomato purée
1 teaspoon crushed mustard seeds
1 teaspoon chilli powder
½ teaspoon ground turmeric
4 green chillies, roughly chopped
200ml (7fl oz) white vinegar
1 teaspoon brown sugar
sea salt

1   Heat the oil in a large, non-stick frying pan. Add the fenugreek seeds and cook, stirring constantly, for 1 minute or until they turn golden. Add the garlic and cook gently, stirring occasionally, for about 5 minutes until it is tender and has started to colour.

2   Add the tomato purée, mustard seeds, chilli powder, turmeric, chillies and a little salt. Fry the mixture for 2–3 minutes, then pour in the vinegar and cook over a low heat for about 25–30 minutes until the garlic is browned and all the liquid has evaporated.

3   Stir in the sugar, then remove the pan from the heat and set aside to cool before use or storage. You can keep the pickle sealed in a screw-top jar in the fridge for up to 2 weeks.

shrimp pickle

This recipe is a contribution from a fishing family living in Cochin, South India, where fresh seafood is eaten at least twice a day. The people of Cochin are said to make the best fish dishes in the world, slipping their fresh catch of the day straight into the pan along with traditional smoky tamarind and sun-dried, red hot chillies. The pickle was devised as a means of survival during the monsoon and other rough times when fishermen were unable to put their boats out to sea. If shrimp are hard to find, use small peeled prawns instead.

SERVES 4

1cm (1/2 inch) piece fresh root ginger, peeled and chopped
2 garlic cloves, peeled
1/2 teaspoon ground turmeric
1 teaspoon sea salt
200g (7oz) peeled shrimp, chopped

vegetable oil for deep-frying, plus 4 tablespoons
1/2 teaspoon mustard seeds
few curry leaves
2 green chillies, slit lengthways
1 teaspoon chilli powder
1 teaspoon mustard powder
300ml (1/2 pint) white wine vinegar

1 Using a small spice mill or a mortar and pestle, pound the chopped ginger and garlic together to make a paste. Set aside.

2 In a small bowl, mix together the turmeric and salt with 1 tablespoon water to make a paste. Add the chopped shrimp and stir to coat.

3 Heat a 5cm (2 inch) depth of oil in a large, heavy-based saucepan or wok to 180–190°C or until a cube of bread browns in 30 seconds. Deep-fry the shrimp for 3–4 minutes until light golden, then remove with a slotted spoon and set aside to drain on kitchen paper.

4 Heat 4 tablespoons oil in a large frying pan. Add the mustard seeds and, when they start to pop, add the curry leaves, chillies, chilli powder, mustard powder and the ginger-garlic paste. Cook, stirring constantly, for 1 minute, or until the spices give off a toasted aroma.

5 Add the shrimp and cook, stirring constantly, for a further 2–3 minutes or until all the pieces are coated with the spice mixture. Pour in the wine vinegar and simmer, stirring occasionally, for 10 minutes or until the pickle thickens. Remove the pan from the heat and set aside to cool before serving.

starters, snacks and chutneys   **29**

coconut chutney

There is nothing like a freshly made, tangy, spiced chutney to accompany special snacks, curries and rice dishes. Made with fresh coconut, this chutney has a good, sharp, clean flavour.

SERVES 4

1 tablespoon tamarind pulp
100g (3½oz) freshly grated coconut
2 green chillies, roughly chopped
2.5cm (1 inch) piece fresh root ginger, peeled
   and sliced

1 garlic clove, peeled
2 tablespoons vegetable oil
1 teaspoon mustard seeds
1 small onion, peeled and finely chopped
10 curry leaves
sea salt

1 Break up the tamarind pulp and place in a small bowl. Add 3 tablespoons hot water and leave to soak for 20–30 minutes. Press the mixture through a sieve to extract 3 tablespoons of tamarind liquid and pour this into a blender. Add the coconut, chillies, ginger, garlic and a little salt, and process to a smooth paste.

2 Heat the oil in a small frying pan. Add the mustard seeds and, when they start to pop, stir in the onion and curry leaves. Cook over a medium heat for 2–3 minutes or until the onion is golden. Lower the heat and add the coconut mixture. Mix well and serve hot or cold.

kiwi fruit chutney

As I adore fresh chutneys, I enjoy experimenting with different fruits and vegetables to extend my repertoire. Kiwi fruit, with its sweet-sour flavour, has the ideal qualities for a delicious chutney. Try this recipe with other fruits too.

SERVES 4

200g (7oz) kiwi fruit
1 tomato, finely chopped
2 green chillies, chopped
3 shallots, peeled and chopped

1cm (½ inch) piece fresh root ginger, peeled
   and very finely chopped
pinch of freshly ground black pepper
sea salt

1 Peel the kiwi fruit and cut the flesh into small pieces. Place the tomato, chillies, shallots, ginger, black pepper and a little salt in a blender and pulse briefly until the tomatoes are just lightly crushed.

2 Add the kiwi fruit a little at a time, processing slowly until you have a coarse textured chutney. Transfer to a small serving dish.

sweet mango chutney

Made with sweet fruit, this versatile chutney is reminiscent of Bombay and other areas of the Maharashtra state. It tastes very different from the spicy, sour mango chutneys that are typical of my home state, Kerala.

SERVES 4

200g (7oz) sweet mango
25g (1oz) shallot or onion, peeled and chopped
2 green chillies, chopped
2 garlic cloves, peeled
2 tablespoons curry leaves
sea salt

1 Peel the mango, cut the flesh away from the stone, then dice it and set aside. Place the shallot or onion, chillies, garlic, curry leaves and a little salt in a blender and process to a smooth paste. Add the diced mango and process to a coarse paste.

2 Transfer the mango chutney to a serving bowl, cover with cling film and chill in the refrigerator before serving.

date chutney

Dates make a good, rich chutney that goes particularly well with samosas (pages 24–5) and onion bhajis (page 20). Using fresh juicy dates rather than dried ones gives a truly succulent dip.

SERVES 4

200g (7oz) fresh dates, chopped
3 garlic cloves, peeled and chopped
2 dried red chillies
4 tablespoons lime juice
2 tablespoons freshly grated coconut
sea salt

1 Place the dates, garlic, chillies, lime juice and coconut in a blender and process to a smooth paste. Transfer to a serving bowl.

2 soups, salads and side dishes

Keralan seafood soup

This exquisite soup combines three things Kerala is particularly renowned for – spices, coconuts and seafood – and it can be varied to include any fresh seafood. It is rich in flavour, and makes a substantial dish thanks to the inclusion of rice. Jamie Oliver says it's one of the best soups he has ever had in his life. I recommend you serve it with bread, preferably appams (pages 158–9) or parathas (pages 155–6).

SERVES 4

50g (2oz) long-grain white rice

4 tablespoons vegetable oil

1 teaspoon mustard seeds

pinch of cumin seeds

20 curry leaves, chopped

4 garlic cloves, peeled and chopped

2.5cm (1 inch) piece fresh root ginger, peeled and chopped

3 green chillies, finely sliced

3 onions, peeled and chopped

1/2 teaspoon ground turmeric

1/2 teaspoon chilli powder

1/2 teaspoon crushed black pepper

250g (9oz) raw prawns, peeled, deveined and halved if large

200ml (7fl oz) coconut milk

TO SERVE:

4 cooked king prawns in shell (optional)

3 tablespoons freshly grated coconut

1 Cook the rice in 350ml (12fl oz) water in a small saucepan. When the rice is just tender, drain and reserve 250ml (8fl oz) of the cooking water. Set aside.

2 Heat the oil in a medium saucepan. Add the mustard seeds and, when they start to pop, add the cumin seeds, curry leaves, garlic, ginger, chillies and onions. Fry for 5 minutes or until the onions are soft. Stir in the turmeric, chilli powder and black pepper, and stir-fry for 2 minutes.

3 Add the prawns, cooked rice and the reserved cooking water. Cook over a low heat for 10 minutes or until the prawns are cooked and the soup is creamy. Add the coconut milk, bring to the boil, then lower the heat and simmer for a further 5 minutes.

4 Ladle the seafood soup into warmed bowls and top each serving with a whole cooked prawn if you like. Scatter with freshly grated coconut and serve.

spiced lentil soup

Soups aren't something you come across very often in India, as they're not part of the traditional food culture, but increasingly they are offered as a first course on restaurant menus. This one is based on a spiced mixture of lentils and beans, and is the ideal winter warmer. Green pepper and spinach help make it colourful, and you can add potatoes to make it more filling if you prefer.

SERVES 4

125g (4oz) split red lentils
50g (2oz) chana dal, or yellow split peas
50g (2oz) mung beans
1 onion, peeled and finely sliced
1 tomato, diced
1 green pepper, cored, deseeded and diced
50g (2oz) spinach leaves, tough stalks removed
4 garlic cloves, peeled and finely chopped
2 green chillies, finely sliced
2.5cm (1 inch) piece fresh root ginger, peeled and finely chopped
1 teaspoon chilli powder
1 teaspoon garam masala
1 teaspoon ground turmeric
sea salt
4 tablespoons coriander leaves, finely chopped, to serve

1 Combine the lentils, chana dal, mung beans, onion, tomato, green pepper, spinach, garlic, chillies, ginger, chilli powder, garam masala, turmeric and a little salt in a saucepan.

2 Stir in 1.2 litres (2 pints) water and bring to the boil. Simmer, stirring frequently, for 20 minutes or until the pulses are thoroughly cooked.

3 Ladle the soup into warmed bowls and sprinkle chopped coriander leaves over each portion. Serve hot, with Indian bread if you like.

spicy mixed salad

Just like anywhere else in the world, salads are popular in India, but they are usually spiked with some chilli. This recipe is very flexible – vary the spices, vegetables and fruit to taste.

SERVES 4

3 tomatoes
1/2 cucumber
2 apples
2 pears
2 oranges
2 bananas, peeled
50g (2oz) radishes, quartered
pinch of garam masala
1 1/2 teaspoons sea salt
1/2 teaspoon chilli powder
2 tablespoons lemon juice

1 Cut the tomatoes, cucumber, apples and pears into bite-sized chunks and place in a large bowl. Peel and segment the oranges, then halve each segment and add to the bowl. Cut the bananas into chunks and toss them into the salad with the quartered radishes.

2 Sprinkle the garam masala, salt and chilli powder over the salad, then add the lemon juice and toss well. Cover and chill slightly before serving.

paw paw salad

In India, the tropical paw paw (also known as papaya) is included in curries, stir-fries and spicy dishes, such as this refreshing salad.

SERVES 4

1 small, ripe paw paw
1 guava
1 tablespoon vegetable oil
1/2 teaspoon urad dal
8 shallots, peeled and finely sliced
pinch of chilli powder
4 tablespoons wine or cider vinegar
pinch of sea salt
5 tablespoons coconut milk
juice of 1 lemon

1 Peel, halve and deseed the paw paw and guava, then cut into cubes. Set aside in a large bowl.

2 Heat the oil in a frying pan. Add the urad dal and fry, stirring, for 1–2 minutes until it turns brown, then add the shallots and sauté over a low heat for 1 minute. Sprinkle in the chilli powder, then add the vinegar and salt. Increase the heat and stir-fry for 1 minute. Remove the pan from the heat and slowly mix in the coconut milk.

3 Pour the shallot mixture over the prepared fruits, add the lemon juice and toss well. Serve cold.

coconut and radish salad

This salad is wonderfully quick to make and has a lovely clean, fresh flavour, with a nutty crunch provided by the toasted urad dal. You can use cucumber instead of radishes, if you prefer.

SERVES 4

2 tablespoons vegetable oil
1 teaspoon mustard seeds
1 teaspoon urad dal
few curry leaves
100g (3¹/₂oz) shallots, peeled and halved
3 green chillies, finely chopped
3 tablespoons lemon juice
3 tablespoons white wine vinegar
50g (2oz) freshly grated coconut
200g (7oz) radishes, quartered
sea salt

1 Heat the oil in a large frying pan or wok. Add the mustard seeds and, when they start to pop, add the urad dal and curry leaves. Cook, stirring constantly, for 1–2 minutes until the urad dal turns brown.

2 Add the shallots and stir-fry for 5 minutes or until they are shiny and translucent. Add the chillies and a little salt and stir-fry for 1 minute. Pour in the lemon juice and vinegar, then add the grated coconut and mix well. Remove the pan from the heat.

3 Transfer the fried mixture to a large bowl. Add the quartered radishes and toss to mix, then serve.

tomato and red onion raita

In India I knew raita simply as an accompaniment to *Hyderabadi biryani*, but since moving to London, I have realised that it is a very important item on every Indian restaurant menu. Raita helps cool the effect of those fiery dishes that can take you by surprise, so many British people order it as a matter of routine when having an Indian meal. Red onions work fine in such a dish, because they are milder and sweeter than ordinary onions.

SERVES 4

1cm (1/2 inch) piece fresh root ginger
3 green chillies
1 red onion, peeled
1 tomato

50g (2oz) cucumber
200g (7oz) yogurt

TO SERVE:
pinch of chilli powder
chopped coriander leaves (optional)

1 Peel and very finely chop the ginger. The easiest way to do this is to remove the skin with a swivel vegetable peeler, then cut the ginger into thin slices. Cut these slices into matchsticks, then into tiny dice.

2 Finely slice the green chilli into rings. Chop the red onion very finely. Cut the tomato and cucumber into tiny cubes, discarding the seeds.

3 Put the yogurt in a large bowl. Add the tomato, cucumber, red onion, chillies and ginger and stir to mix. Serve sprinkled with a pinch of chilli powder and chopped coriander leaves if you like.

thoran

Thorans are lightly cooked vegetable salads that appear at nearly every Keralan meal to provide a fresh-tasting, crunchy contrast to saucy dishes. We often describe them as dry dishes, but the balance they bring to a meal is healthy and textural. Thorans' unique mild and nutty flavours are derived from fried urad dal, curry leaves and freshly grated coconut – the most important ingredient. Onion or shallot is usually included, and sometimes cashew nuts for extra crunch.

The basic thoran cooking technique is reminiscent of Chinese stir-frying. It suits most firm vegetables, but thoran can also be made with tougher leafy greens, such as cabbage, and starchy foods, like cooked pulses, potato and plantain. The vegetables may be par-cooked before stir-frying, but most often they are cut into small pieces and added straight to the pan. In Kerala we use whatever vegetables are in season. Try the following thorans – each serves 4–6.

▲ shallot thoran

Heat 5 tbsp oil in a pan. Add 1 tsp mustard seeds and, when they start to pop, add 1 tsp urad dal and 10 curry leaves. Cook, stirring, for 1–2 minutes or until the dal turns brown. Add 250g (9oz) finely chopped shallots, 3 finely chopped green chillies and a little salt, and cook for 5 minutes or until the shallots are transparent. Mix in 100g (3½oz) freshly grated coconut and a few extra curry leaves and stir-fry for 1 minute. Serve immediately.

white cabbage thoran

Heat 5 tbsp oil in a pan. Fry 1½ tbsp mustard seeds until they pop. Add 10 curry leaves and 1 tsp urad dal. Cook, stirring, for 1–2 minutes until the dal browns. Add 3 finely sliced onions and 4 dried red chillies. Cook on a high heat for 1 minute, then gently until the onions are soft. Add salt and 1 tsp turmeric. Stir in 1 small shredded cabbage; cook, covered, for 15 minutes or until tender. Stir in 100g (3½oz) grated coconut and serve.

green bean thoran

Heat 5 tbsp oil in a pan. Fry 1 tsp mustard seeds until they pop. Add 10 curry leaves and 1 tsp urad dal. Cook, stirring, for 1–2 minutes until the dal turns brown. Add 1 finely sliced small onion and 2 diced green chillies. Cook on a high heat for 1 minute, then lower the heat and cook for 5 minutes or until the onion is soft. Stir in 1 tsp turmeric and a little salt. Add 250g (9oz) chopped green beans and cook, covered, for 15–20 minutes until tender. Stir in 50g (2oz) grated coconut and serve.

▲ Savoy cabbage and carrot thoran

Pound 2 diced green chillies, 1 tbsp chopped ginger and 3 garlic cloves with 1 tomato. Heat 5 tbsp oil in a pan, fry 1 tsp mustard seeds until they pop, then add 1 tsp urad dal and cook, stirring, until brown. Add 2 finely sliced onions and 10 curry leaves; cook until soft. Add the chilli mixture; stir for 1 minute. Add 2 shredded carrots, 400g (14oz) shredded Savoy cabbage and 3 tbsp water, cover and cook for 10 minutes. Stir in 200g (7oz) grated coconut, cook for 2 minutes and serve.

okra masala

Widely known as bhindi or ladies' fingers, okra is a favourite vegetable in India, prized for its unusual flavour and texture, whether it is cooked in a tomato and onion masala in the Northern style as in this recipe, or in a crunchy South Indian thoran. You have to be careful when using okra because it doesn't handle heat well and needs to be cooked briefly. Choose relatively small specimens as large ones tend to have large seeds and can be very stringy, even after cooking. I love to eat this okra masala with two chapattis (page 154) – a perfect dinner for me. You can, of course, serve it with other Indian breads, or toasted poppadoms if you prefer.

Illustrated on previous page

SERVES 4

3 tablespoons vegetable oil
pinch of fenugreek seeds
pinch of fennel seeds
2–3 cardamom pods
2.5cm (1 inch) piece cinnamon stick
1 bay leaf
3 garlic cloves, peeled and chopped
3 onions, peeled and finely chopped
1/2 teaspoon ground turmeric
1/2 teaspoon chilli powder
1 teaspoon ground coriander
1 teaspoon tomato purée
2 tomatoes, finely chopped
200g (7oz) okra
coriander leaves, to serve

1 Heat the oil in a medium saucepan, karahi or wok. Add the fenugreek seeds, fennel seeds, cardamom pods, cinnamon stick, bay leaf, garlic and onions, and cook, stirring occasionally, for about 10 minutes until the onions are golden.

2 Add the turmeric, chilli powder, ground coriander and tomato purée, stir well and cook for a further minute. Add the chopped tomatoes and 600ml (1 pint) water, then bring to the boil and simmer for about 10 minutes until the sauce is thick.

3 Meanwhile, top and tail the okra and cut into 1cm (1/2 inch) pieces. Stir the okra into the masala sauce, then cover and cook over a low heat for 5 minutes or until the okra is tender. Serve garnished with coriander leaves.

aubergine stir-fry

Aubergine is considered a highly versatile vegetable in India and is available in an amazing array of colours, sizes and flavours. This is an easy way to enhance it, and uses just a few ingredients.

SERVES 4

4 tablespoons vegetable oil
1 teaspoon mustard seeds
1 onion, peeled and thinly sliced
few curry leaves
1 green chilli, slit lengthways
500g (1lb 2oz) aubergines, cubed

1   Heat the oil in a large frying pan or wok. Add the mustard seeds and, when they start to pop, add the onion and curry leaves and cook for 5 minutes or until the onion is soft.

2   Add the chilli and aubergine cubes and stir well. Cover and cook gently for 5 minutes, then remove the lid and stir-fry for 5 minutes or until the aubergines are tender. Serve hot.

green bean stir-fry

A speedy, light side dish such as this one is an excellent way to add a healthy component to a rich curry meal. You can use any variety of green bean – choose whichever looks freshest.

SERVES 4

250g (9oz) green beans, trimmed
2 tablespoons vegetable oil
1 teaspoon mustard seeds
2 onions, peeled and finely chopped
few curry leaves
3 green chillies, slit lengthways
large pinch of ground turmeric
sea salt

1   Cut the beans into 2.5cm (1 inch) pieces. Heat the oil in a large frying pan or wok and fry the mustard seeds until they start to pop. Add the onions and curry leaves and cook for 4–5 minutes or until the onions are soft. Add the chillies, turmeric and a little salt and sauté for 1 minute.

2   Add the beans, sprinkle in a few tablespoons of water, cover and cook for 5 minutes or until just tender. Remove the lid and stir-fry for 5 minutes or until the dish is dry and crunchy. Serve hot.

green pepper stir-fry

I was introduced to peppers in North India, where they are known as *shimla mirch*. The region has some unforgettable dishes based on them. Peppers bring a lot of colour to dishes, whether they are used raw, grilled, or made into a stir-fry such as this one. Tomatoes and onions are included here, and the result is an ideal accompaniment for saucy dishes.

SERVES 4

300g (11oz) green peppers
4 tablespoons vegetable oil
1/2 teaspoon cumin seeds
2 onions, peeled and finely sliced
2 green chillies, slit lengthways
2.5cm (1 inch) piece fresh root ginger, peeled
  and finely sliced
1/2 teaspoon ground turmeric
1 teaspoon ground coriander
2 tomatoes, finely chopped
2 tablespoons finely chopped coriander leaves,
  to serve

1 Halve, core and deseed the green peppers, then slice finely into long strips. Heat the oil in a large frying pan or wok. Add the cumin seeds, then the onions, chillies and ginger. Cook, stirring occasionally, for 5 minutes or until the onions are soft.

2 Add the turmeric and ground coriander and cook for a further minute before adding the tomatoes. Stir well, then add the green peppers. Sprinkle a few tablespoons of water over the ingredients in the pan and cook for 5 minutes, stirring constantly, until the peppers are soft.

3 Transfer to a large serving dish, sprinkle with chopped coriander leaves and serve hot.

baby corn and carrot stir-fry

Last year I started cooking daily for my colleagues because I wanted to encourage them to eat healthily. One day, as I was shopping in the supermarket, I was drawn to the display of baby vegetables and realised that they could be combined to make the perfect crunchy vegetable side dish. Everyone loves this recipe and, since its inception, there is not another dish that I have prepared as often.

SERVES 4

100g (3¹/₂oz) baby corn,
100g (3¹/₂oz) baby carrots, halved
2 tablespoons vegetable oil
2 onions, peeled and sliced lengthways
2.5cm (1 inch) piece fresh root ginger, peeled
   and finely shredded

2 garlic cloves, peeled and chopped
¹/₂ teaspoon ground turmeric
¹/₂ teaspoon chilli powder
¹/₂ teaspoon garam masala
sea salt
2 tablespoons chopped coriander leaves,
   to serve

1 Cut the baby corn lengthways into quarters. Halve the baby carrots lengthways. Set aside.

2 Heat the oil in a large frying pan. Add the onions, ginger and garlic, and cook, stirring occasionally, for 5 minutes or until the onions are golden brown.

3 Add the turmeric, chilli powder and garam masala and cook, stirring, for a further minute. Stir in the baby corn and carrots, then sprinkle with a few tablespoons of water and add a pinch of salt. Cook for 5 minutes, so that the vegetables are cooked, but still crunchy.

4 Remove the pan from the heat and scatter the coriander leaves over the stir-fry before serving.

spicy new potatoes with spinach

During the new potato season, my wife Alison insisted that I make her a spicy dish with baby new potatoes. I agreed on one condition: that I would be able to add my favourite vegetable, spinach, to it. We both loved the combination. Medium new potatoes work just as well.

SERVES 4

350g (12oz) small or medium new potatoes

2 teaspoons ground turmeric

2 tablespoons vegetable oil

1 teaspoon mustard seeds

1 teaspoon urad dal

2.5cm (1 inch) piece fresh root ginger, peeled and finely chopped

1 green chilli, sliced

1 large onion, peeled and chopped

1 teaspoon chilli powder

2 tomatoes, chopped

250g (9oz) baby leaf spinach

juice of 1/2 lemon

sea salt

1   Place the new potatoes in a large saucepan, cover generously with water and add 1/2 teaspoon turmeric and a little salt. Bring to the boil, cover and cook for 15 minutes or until the potatoes are tender. Drain and set aside.

2   Heat the oil in a large frying pan. Add the mustard seeds then, when they start to pop, add the urad dal, ginger and chilli, and stir-fry for 30 seconds. Add the onion and continue stir-frying until it is softened and light golden. Mix in the chilli powder, the remaining turmeric and a little salt, and stir-fry for a further minute.

3   Add the tomatoes and cook, stirring constantly, for 5 minutes or until they break down. Cover the pan and cook for a further 2 minutes, stirring frequently.

4   Add the spinach and cook, stirring constantly, for 5 minutes or until wilted. Lower the heat, add the drained potatoes and lemon juice and stir thoroughly to combine. Serve hot.

spinach and coconut

This is a re-creation of my mother's best spinach dish, which she used to make with a red leaf variety. You won't believe the difference freshly grated coconut and green chillies make to spinach. Use as much coconut as you like – the taste will only get better. I like to eat this with plain boiled rice and my yogurt curry sauce – basic moru kachiathu (page 89).

SERVES 4

100g (3½oz) freshly grated coconut
3 green chillies, chopped
4 tablespoons vegetable oil
1 teaspoon mustard seeds
1 teaspoon urad dal
10 curry leaves
2 onions, peeled and finely chopped
1 teaspoon ground turmeric
300g (11oz) spinach leaves, chopped
sea salt

1 Place the grated coconut and chopped green chillies in a blender with 250ml (8fl oz) water and process to a coarse paste. Set aside.

2 Heat the oil in a medium saucepan or wok. Add the mustard seeds and, when they start to pop, add the urad dal and curry leaves. Stir-fry for 1–2 minutes or until the urad dal turns brown. Add the onions and stir-fry for 5 minutes or until soft.

3 Stir in the turmeric and a little salt and mix well, then add the chopped spinach leaves. Cover and cook for 5 minutes. Add the coconut paste and stir well. Lower the heat and cook gently for a further 5 minutes, stirring occasionally. Serve hot.

stuffed peppers

White radish isn't very common in India, but I find the combination of strong-flavoured white radish and sweet-tasting peppers excellent. Chick peas help to make this a substantial side dish that can be served with Malabar parathas (page 155) as a healthy lunch or light supper. For an attractive starter, use a selection of different coloured peppers.

SERVES 6

3 peppers

FOR THE STUFFING:
3 tablespoons vegetable oil
1/2 teaspoon cumin seeds
2 garlic cloves, peeled and chopped
2 onions, peeled and finely chopped
1/4 teaspoon ground turmeric

1/2 teaspoon chilli powder
1/2 teaspoon garam masala
150g (5oz) large white radishes, thinly sliced
150g canned chick peas, drained
2 tomatoes, finely chopped
2 tablespoons chopped coriander leaves
sea salt

1 Preheat the oven to 200°C (fan oven 180°C) gas mark 6. Carefully slice off the tops of the peppers and reserve to use as lids. Scrape out the seeds from the pepper cavities. Oil a small baking dish that will hold the peppers upright during baking, using 1 tablespoon oil.

2 Heat 2 tablespoons oil in a large frying pan, karahi or wok. Add the cumin seeds, garlic and onions and fry for 5 minutes or until the onions are soft. Sprinkle in the turmeric, chilli powder, garam masala and a little salt and stir well.

3 Add the radishes, chick peas and tomatoes, and cook for 5 minutes, stirring frequently. Remove the pan from the heat and allow to cool slightly.

4 Fill the pepper cavities with the radish and chick pea mixture and replace the tops. Place them upright in the oiled baking dish, sprinkle with 3 tablespoons of water and roast for 20 minutes or until the peppers are tender.

5 Carefully remove the lids from the peppers and scatter with chopped coriander leaves. Serve hot, halving the peppers lengthways as you serve them.

3 pulses, cheese and eggs

mung bean curry

This dish is popular with the agricultural community of Kerala and is regularly served at lunchtime with a dish of watery rice. It satisfies the hungry farmer after a hard morning's work in the sun and it's a good source of water. We also serve mung bean curry at breakfast with steamed rice cakes. You can vary this dish by adding green bananas instead of potatoes.

SERVES 4

150g (5oz) freshly grated coconut
2 green chillies
250g (9oz) mung beans
1 teaspoon chilli powder
1/2 teaspoon ground turmeric
2 potatoes, peeled and diced
4 tablespoons vegetable oil
1 teaspoon mustard seeds
few curry leaves
3 dried red chillies

1 Place the coconut, green chillies and 250ml (8fl oz) water in a blender and process to a coarse paste. Set aside.

2 Put the mung beans in a saucepan with 750ml (1¼ pints) water. Add the chilli powder and turmeric and bring to the boil, then cover and cook for 20 minutes. Mix in the diced potatoes and continue simmering for a further 10–12 minutes or until the beans and potatoes are cooked.

3 Lower the heat and add the coconut and chilli paste. Stir well, then continue to simmer for a few minutes over a low heat.

4 Meanwhile, heat the oil in a small frying pan. Add the mustard seeds and, when they start to pop, add the curry leaves and the dried chillies. Pour the contents of the pan over the cooked mung beans, toss well and serve hot.

spinach and chick pea curry

Chick pea dishes are common in North India, where this pulse is a local crop and available in a surprising array of colours and shapes. The strong flavour of garam masala complements the rich taste of chick peas exceptionally well, and spinach imparts colour and flavour. You can serve this curry with any Indian bread.

SERVES 4

1 green chilli, deseeded and chopped
2.5cm (1 inch) piece fresh root ginger, peeled
  and finely chopped
2 tablespoons vegetable oil
2 garlic cloves, peeled and sliced
1 onion, peeled and finely chopped
¼ teaspoon chilli powder

¼ teaspoon ground turmeric
½ teaspoon ground coriander
2 teaspoons tomato purée
400g (14oz) spinach leaves, tough stalks
  removed
410g can chick peas, drained and rinsed
sea salt

1 Using a pestle and mortar, finely grind the chilli and ginger together, adding a spoonful of water to help make a paste. Set aside.

2 Heat the oil in a large frying pan. Add the garlic and stir-fry for 30 seconds, then add the onion and cook, stirring constantly, for about 5 minutes until it is soft and lightly golden at the edges. Add the chilli powder, turmeric, ground coriander and tomato purée, and stir-fry for 2 minutes.

3 Pour 300ml (½ pint) water into the pan and bring to the boil. Stir in the spinach and chick peas, with a pinch of salt. Cook, stirring occasionally, for 5 minutes or until they are well blended with the spices and the spinach has wilted. Serve hot.

chick pea curry

A Punjabi friend from Delhi gave me the idea for this recipe. Keralans are used to eating chick pea curries with roasted coconut sauce, but here I have tried to combine North and South Indian styles to create a unique flavour. The strong flavour of the spice blend, married with the creamy texture of coconut milk, makes it rather like a masala sauce. It is best served with a mild side dish.

SERVES 4–6

4 tablespoons vegetable oil
2.5cm (1 inch) piece cinnamon stick
2 cloves
3 cardamom pods, crushed
pinch of fennel seeds
4 garlic cloves, peeled and chopped
2.5cm (1 inch) piece fresh root ginger,
    finely chopped
2 green chillies, finely chopped
3 onions, peeled and chopped

1/2 teaspoon ground turmeric
1 teaspoon chilli powder
1 1/2 teaspoons ground coriander
1/2 teaspoon garam masala
1 teaspoon tomato purée
4 tomatoes, chopped
2 x 410g cans chick peas, drained and rinsed
200ml (7 fl oz) coconut milk
sea salt
4 tablespoons chopped coriander leaves,
    to serve

1 Heat the oil in a saucepan. Add the cinnamon stick, cloves, cardamoms, fennel seeds, garlic, ginger and chillies, and sauté for 1 minute. Add the onions and fry over a medium heat for 15–20 minutes or until they are soft and golden.

2 Add the turmeric, chilli powder, ground coriander, garam masala, tomato purée and salt. Mix well, then add the chopped tomatoes and 600ml (1 pint) water. Bring to the boil and add the chick peas. Cover and cook over a medium heat for 15 minutes, stirring occasionally.

3 Lower the heat and add the coconut milk. Simmer gently for 5 minutes or until the milk is well blended with the spices and chick peas. Remove the pan from the heat, scatter with chopped coriander leaves and serve hot.

kidney bean curry

Kidney beans are typical of North Indian states and are particularly prominent during festivals and other big occasions. Traditionally dried beans are used, making this a time consuming dish to prepare. Here I simmer canned beans with spices and tomato, enriching the curry with cream before serving. You could also add spinach or potatoes to enhance the colour and flavour, if you like. Serve the curry with chapattis (page 154) or Malabar parathas (page 155).

SERVES 4–6

3 tablespoons vegetable oil
1 teaspoon cumin seeds
5 garlic cloves, peeled and chopped
3 onions, peeled and sliced
2.5cm (1 inch) piece fresh root ginger, peeled
  and grated
1 teaspoon chilli powder
1 teaspoon ground coriander
1 teaspoon garam masala
1/2 teaspoon ground turmeric
5 tomatoes, chopped
410g can kidney beans, drained and rinsed
4 tablespoons double cream
5 tablespoons chopped coriander leaves,
  to serve

1   Heat the oil in a large saucepan. Add the cumin seeds and garlic, and cook briefly until the garlic is golden. Add the onions and ginger and cook, stirring occasionally, for 10 minutes or until the onions are softened and golden.

2   Stir in the chilli powder, ground coriander, garam masala and turmeric. Add the tomatoes and kidney beans and cook, stirring constantly, for 1 minute. Pour in 400ml (14 fl oz) water and bring the mixture to the boil. Lower the heat, cover and simmer for 20 minutes or until the beans are soft.

3   Remove from the heat and stir in the cream. Scatter with chopped coriander leaves to serve.

dals

For millions of Indian people, dal – a thick, soupy dish of lentils or other pulses – is the most important dish they eat, and an essential source of vegetarian protein. In North Indian villages a nutritious meal of dal and chapatti can be served any time of day. In the South, people are more inclined to eat dal with rice. Although based on humble ingredients, dal is also served on auspicious occasions, such as wedding feasts.

Most Indian restaurants in Britain offer only one or two dals, which often taste remarkably similar, yet on the Indian sub-continent, dals are varied according to local customs, seasons and events. Different spices and lentils are combined to give dals of varying thickness and smoothness, some mild and sweet, others hot in flavour.

The dals featured here are my favourites, inspired by those I have eaten in Delhi, and made with pulses available here. They are varied in texture and taste; each serves 4–6.

▲ lentil and spinach dal
Put 100g (3½oz) split red lentils, 50g (2oz) mung beans, 50g (2oz) chana dal or split peas, 1 chopped potato, 3 diced onions, 3 diced green chillies, 3 chopped tomatoes, 1 tsp turmeric, 1 tsp chilli powder and 650ml (1 pint 2fl oz) water in a pan. Simmer, covered, for 15 minutes or until tender. Add 100g (3½oz) spinach leaves and cook for 5 minutes. Heat 4 tbsp oil in a pan, briefly fry ¼ tsp cumin seeds with 3 finely chopped garlic cloves, then pour over the dal to serve.

red lentil dal

Place 200g (7oz) split red lentils, 2 finely sliced onions, 3 diced tomatoes, 4 finely sliced garlic cloves, 1 tbsp finely diced ginger, 1 tsp chilli powder, 1 tsp ground coriander, $^{1}/_{2}$ tsp turmeric, a little salt and 1.2 litres (2 pints) water in a pan. Simmer, covered for 20 minutes or until tender; cook uncovered for 5 minutes. Heat 4 tbsp oil in a pan and fry 1 tsp mustard seeds until they pop. Add 10 curry leaves, stir briefly and pour over the dal.

mung bean and coconut dal

Whiz 50g (2oz) freshly grated coconut, a pinch of cumin seeds and 250ml (8fl oz) water to a paste in a blender. Place 200g (7oz) mung beans in a pan with 1.2 litres (2 pints) water, 2 finely chopped green chillies, $^{1}/_{2}$ tsp turmeric and a little salt. Simmer, covered, for 15 minutes or until tender. Add the coconut paste and cook for 5 minutes. Lower the heat and add 200ml (7fl oz) coconut milk and a few curry leaves. Simmer for 5 minutes, then serve.

▲ tarka dal

Place 200g (7oz) split red lentils, 50g (2oz) chana dal or split peas, 2 finely sliced onions, 2 diced tomatoes, 2 finely chopped garlic cloves, 2 sliced green chillies, 1 tsp chilli powder, 1 tsp turmeric, salt and 1.5 litres (2$^{1}/_{2}$ pints) water in a pan. Simmer, covered, for 20 minutes or until the lentils are tender. Cook uncovered for 5 minutes. Heat 2 tbsp oil in a frying pan, sauté 4 shredded garlic cloves and $^{1}/_{2}$ tsp cumin seeds for 1 minute, then pour over the dal. Top with chopped coriander to serve.

fried paneer with tomato and shallot chutney

Paneer dishes are now popular all over India, although they originated in the Punjab and other parts of North India. Paneer is an unusual cheese because it can be fried without a protective coating and stays firm, however, you must ensure that the oil is very hot so that the cheese colours quickly. I developed this dish to bring together the full flavour of the cheese with a refreshing shallot and tomato chutney.

SERVES 2–4

150g (5oz) paneer cheese
vegetable oil, for deep-frying

FOR THE CHUTNEY:
3 tomatoes, roughly chopped
6 shallots, peeled and roughly chopped
1 green chilli, roughly chopped
2 tablespoons coriander leaves
1 tablespoon lemon juice
pinch of garam masala
sea salt

1 To make the chutney, put the tomatoes, shallots, chilli, coriander leaves and a little salt in a blender and process briefly until the tomatoes and shallots are just crushed. Transfer the mixture to a bowl and add the lemon juice and garam masala. Set aside.

2 Cut the paneer into large cubes. Heat the oil for deep-frying in a large, heavy-based saucepan, karahi or wok to 180°–190°C or until a cube of bread browns in 30 seconds. Deep-fry the paneer for 1–2 minutes or until lightly browned. Remove with a slotted spoon and drain on kitchen paper.

3 Serve the fried paneer hot or cold, with the tomato and shallot chutney spooned over the top.

green pea and cheese curry

Famously known as *mutter paneer*, this dish appears on most Indian restaurant menus. I am a big fan of it and like to eat it with Malabar parathas (page 155). As paneer cheese and peas are widely available, it's an easy dish to make. You can try cooking it with green or red peppers too.

SERVES 4

150g (5oz) paneer cheese

vegetable oil, for deep-frying

4 tablespoons vegetable oil

3 small onions, peeled and sliced

2.5cm (1 inch) piece fresh root ginger, peeled and finely chopped

1 teaspoon ground coriander

1/2 teaspoon ground cumin

1/2 teaspoon ground turmeric

1/2 teaspoon garam masala

1/2 teaspoon poppy seeds

1 teaspoon tomato purée

100g (31/2oz) peas

4 tablespoons double cream

3 tablespoons chopped coriander leaves (optional)

sea salt

1 Cut the paneer into 1cm (1/2 inch) cubes. Heat the oil for deep-frying in a large, heavy-based saucepan, karahi or wok to 180°–190°C or until a cube of bread browns in 30 seconds. Deep-fry the paneer cubes for 1–2 minutes or until golden, then remove with a slotted spoon and set aside to drain on kitchen paper.

2 Heat 4 tablespoons oil in a saucepan, karahi or wok. Add the onions and ginger and cook, stirring occasionally, for 10 minutes until golden. Add the coriander, cumin, turmeric, garam masala and poppy seeds and cook for 2 minutes. Stir in the tomato purée and continue cooking for a further 3–4 minutes.

3 Pour in 250ml (8fl oz) water and bring the mixture to the boil. Simmer for 5 minutes, then add the peas, fried paneer and some salt and cook for a further 5 minutes.

4 Turn the heat as low as possible and stir in the cream. Cook gently for 2–3 minutes before adding the chopped coriander leaves if using. Serve hot, with a flat bread.

spinach and paneer

Palak paneer, as this dish is known in North India, is one of those wholesome vegetarian dishes that is usually enjoyed by meat-eaters too. The crisp, chewy pieces of paneer go extraordinarily well with soft spiced spinach, and the creamy texture of the sauce makes it an excellent accompaniment to stronger dishes.

SERVES 4

175ml (6 fl oz) vegetable oil
50g (2oz) paneer cheese, cubed
1/2 teaspoon cumin seeds
4 garlic cloves, peeled and chopped
2 onions, peeled and diced
2 green chillies, finely chopped
5 curry leaves
250g (9oz) spinach leaves, finely chopped
1 teaspoon ground turmeric
1 teaspoon chilli powder
1 teaspoon garam masala
1 teaspoon ground coriander
2 tomatoes, finely chopped
1 green pepper, cored, deseeded and cubed
3 1/2 tablespoons single cream
125ml (4fl oz) milk
sea salt

1 Heat 125ml (4fl oz) vegetable oil in a deep frying pan. Add the paneer cubes and cook, turning occasionally, for 1–2 minutes or until lightly browned all over. Remove the pan from the heat, lift out the paneer cubes with a slotted spoon and set aside to drain on kitchen paper.

2 Heat the remaining 4 tablespoons oil in a large saucepan. Add the cumin seeds and garlic and cook, stirring, for 1–2 minutes until golden. Add the onions, chillies and curry leaves and cook, stirring occasionally, for 5 minutes or until the onions are soft.

3 Add the spinach, turmeric, chilli powder, garam masala, ground coriander and some salt. Mix well, then add the tomatoes and green pepper. Cook, stirring from time to time, for 5 minutes or until the mixture is reduced slightly and thick.

4 Stir in the cream and milk, then bring the mixture to the boil, stirring constantly. Remove the pan from the heat, stir in the fried paneer and serve.

egg curry

Egg dishes are rarely seen in Indian restaurants in Britain, but they are often made at home in India, especially in rural areas where people tend to keep chickens. Not only do eggs bring protein to meals, they are simple to cook and economical to use. This hard-boiled egg curry is delicious and quick to make.

SERVES 4

6 eggs
3 tablespoons vegetable oil
1 teaspoon mustard seeds
2 garlic cloves, peeled and chopped
2 dried red chillies
10 curry leaves
1 onion, peeled and very finely sliced
1 teaspoon chilli powder
1/2 teaspoon ground coriander
1/2 teaspoon cumin seeds, crushed
1/2 teaspoon ground turmeric
1 teaspoon tomato purée
5 tomatoes, finely chopped
400ml (14 fl oz) coconut milk
sea salt
2 tablespoons chopped coriander leaves,
  to serve

1 Place the eggs in a large saucepan, cover with water and slowly bring to the boil, then lower the heat and simmer for 10 minutes. Drain and leave to cool in a bowl of cold water. Peel away the shells, rinse the eggs to remove any stray pieces, then set aside.

2 Heat the oil in a medium saucepan. Add the mustard seeds and, when they start to pop, add the garlic, dried chillies and curry leaves and sauté for 1 minute or until the garlic is golden. Add the onion with a good pinch of salt and cook, stirring constantly, for 5 minutes or until it is softened.

3 Stir in the chilli powder, ground coriander, crushed cumin and turmeric, then mix in the tomato purée and chopped tomatoes. Cook for 5 minutes, stirring constantly, until the sauce is well blended.

4 Lower the heat and pour in the coconut milk, stirring to combine. Gently drop the eggs into the sauce and cook gently for a further 5 minutes or until the eggs are hot and the sauce is thick. Scatter with chopped coriander leaves before serving.

egg and onion masala

How can I ever forget my favourite canteen meal from university days? The best-selling dish at lunchtime was always paratha with this delicious egg curry. The masala sauce has a lovely hint of coconut and works well as the base for a dish of spicy potatoes. I have also made this curry with peas instead of eggs, with good results.

SERVES 4

75g (3oz) freshly grated coconut
6 large eggs
3 tablespoons vegetable oil
pinch of fennel seeds
pinch of fenugreek seeds
2 garlic cloves, peeled and finely chopped
4 green chillies, slit lengthways
2.5cm (1 inch) piece fresh root ginger, peeled
   and finely chopped

20 curry leaves
3 small onions, peeled and finely sliced
3 tomatoes, chopped
1/2 teaspoon ground turmeric
1/2 teaspoon chilli powder
sea salt
chopped coriander leaves, to serve

1   Place the grated coconut and 125ml (4fl oz) water in a blender and process until you have a fine paste. Set aside.

2   Place the eggs in a large saucepan, cover with water and slowly bring to the boil, then lower the heat and simmer for 10 minutes. Drain and leave to cool in a bowl of cold water. Peel away the shells, rinse the eggs to remove any stray pieces and set aside.

3   Heat the oil in a large saucepan. Add the fennel and fenugreek seeds and fry until they turn golden, then add the garlic, chillies, ginger and curry leaves and sauté for 2–3 minutes. Add the onions and fry for about 5 minutes until they are softened. Add the tomatoes, turmeric, chilli powder and a little salt and cook for 5 minutes or until the sauce is thick.

4   Lower the heat, stir in the coconut paste and cook for 5 minutes, stirring occasionally. Halve the hard-boiled eggs lengthways and add to the pan. Mix very gently until they are coated with the sauce. Warm through gently, then remove the pan from the heat. Serve hot, scattered with chopped coriander. Accompany with rice or appams (pages 158–9).

Indian scrambled eggs

This dish is essentially a thoran and in India it would be served as part of a substantial meal. However, it is easy enough to make for breakfast or brunch, in which case you need only serve it with bread or rice. The spicing is very simple and light. Using shallots instead of onions helps to keep the flavour mild and sweet.
Illustrated on previous page

SERVES 2
3 large eggs
2 tablespoons vegetable oil
1/2 teaspoon mustard seeds
10 curry leaves
100g (3½oz) shallots, peeled and finely sliced
1/4 teaspoon ground turmeric
1/4 teaspoon chilli powder
1 tomato, chopped
sea salt
1 tablespoon chopped coriander leaves, to serve
  (optional)

1 Break the eggs into a bowl and add a little salt. Whisk with a fork or hand whisk for 1–2 minutes or until well mixed and bubbles start to form on the surface.

2 Heat the oil in a large frying pan. Add the mustard seeds and, when they start to pop, add the curry leaves and stir-fry for 2 minutes or until fragrant. Add the shallots and cook, stirring, over a low heat for 5 minutes or until softened.

3 Stir in the turmeric and chilli powder, then add the tomato and cook gently for 5 minutes. Pour in the beaten eggs and, using a wooden spoon, stir constantly for 3 minutes or so, until they are scrambled. Remove the pan from the heat and scatter lightly with chopped coriander if you like. Serve at once, with plain rice or bread.

spicy eggs with aubergine and spinach

Spicy egg dishes, such as this one, are a favourite with my friend Jamie Oliver, who loves the flavour of chillies. The fiery sauce is beautifully balanced by the use of fresh ginger. An ideal partner would be Muslim-style rice with ghee (page 167), or even plain rice, and don't forget to have a cooling raita or some yogurt on the side.

SERVES 4–6

6 eggs
4 tablespoons vegetable oil
3 onions, peeled and sliced lengthways
3 green chillies, finely chopped
3 garlic cloves, peeled and finely chopped
2.5cm (1 inch) piece fresh root ginger, peeled and
  finely chopped
few curry leaves
1 teaspoon tomato purée
1 teaspoon ground coriander
$1/2$ teaspoon ground turmeric
$1/2$ teaspoon chilli powder
$1/2$ teaspoon garam masala
3 tomatoes, finely sliced
100g ($31/2$oz) baby aubergines, quartered
100g ($31/2$oz) baby spinach leaves
sea salt

1 Place the eggs in a large saucepan, cover with water and slowly bring to the boil, then lower the heat and simmer for 10 minutes. Drain and leave to cool in a bowl of cold water. Peel away the shells, rinse the eggs to remove any stray pieces and set aside.

2 Heat the oil in a frying pan or wok. Add the onions, chillies, garlic, ginger and curry leaves and cook, stirring frequently, for 5 minutes or until the onions are soft. Add the tomato purée, ground coriander, turmeric, chilli powder, garam masala and a little salt. Cook, stirring, for 1 minute.

3 Add the tomatoes, aubergines and spinach leaves. Cover and cook, stirring from time to time, for 6–7 minutes or until the sauce has blended well with the aubergines and spinach.

4 Add the hard-boiled eggs to the pan and allow them to heat through gently in the sauce for about 5 minutes before serving.

4 vegetables

shallot and green banana theeyal

This dish is typical of the Nair community to which I belong and was a family favourite as I was growing up. It can be made with any chunky vegetable, but shallots are essential. I like to serve theeyal with plain rice and a little yogurt, and you'll find it tastes even better the day after making.

SERVES 4

2 green bananas or plantain, peeled

3 tablespoons vegetable oil

250g (9oz) shallots, peeled and quartered

2 green chillies, slit lengthways

1 teaspoon ground turmeric

3 tomatoes, quartered

1/2 teaspoon mustard seeds

10 curry leaves

juice of 1 lime

sea salt

FOR THE SPICED COCONUT LIQUID:

50g (2oz) freshly grated coconut

2 tablespoons coriander seeds

3 dried red chillies

1 garlic clove, peeled

1 cinnamon stick

1   For the spiced coconut liquid, dry-toast all the ingredients in a large frying pan for 4–5 minutes or until the coconut turns brown. Remove the pan from the heat and leave the mixture to cool for 5 minutes. Remove the cinnamon stick, then transfer the mixture to a blender. Add 450ml (3/4 pint) water and process slowly until evenly blended.

2   Cut the bananas into 2.5cm (1 inch) pieces. Heat 2 tablespoons oil in a large saucepan or wok. Add the bananas, shallots and chillies and cook for 5 minutes or until the shallots are softened. Add the turmeric, coconut liquid and a little salt, and cook on a medium heat, stirring occasionally, for 5 minutes.

3   Mix in the tomatoes and cook over a low heat for 10 minutes or until the shallots are very tender. When the curry is nearly ready, heat the remaining 1 tablespoon oil in a frying pan. Add the mustard seeds and, when they start to pop, add the curry leaves. Pour the contents of the frying pan over the curry and stir through. Add the lime juice and cook over a medium heat for 3 minutes before serving.

vegetable and coconut milk stew

Whenever you eat at a South Indian restaurant, a delicious vegetable and coconut milk stew is almost sure to be on the menu. It is one of the mildest dishes in our repertoire and has plenty of sweet-tasting coconut milk sauce, making it ideal for children too. Again, you can vary this dish, as we do all the time, with whatever fresh vegetables you have to hand.
Illustrated on previous page

SERVES 4
1 teaspoon ghee or butter
12 shallots, peeled and cut into wedges
1½ teaspoons plain flour
3 tablespoons tomato purée
½ teaspoon chilli powder
½ teaspoon ground coriander
½ teaspoon ground turmeric
250g (9oz) pumpkin, peeled and cut into batons
200g (7oz) green beans, trimmed
150g (5oz) cauliflower florets
100g (3½oz) peas
250ml (8fl oz) coconut milk
sea salt

1   Heat the ghee or butter in a large saucepan. Add the shallots and fry, stirring, for 5 minutes or until golden. Remove from the heat and sprinkle in the flour. Stir well and return to a low heat.

2   Slowly add 450ml (¾ pint) water, stirring well to prevent any lumps of flour forming. Mix in the tomato purée, chilli powder, ground coriander and turmeric, then add the pumpkin, green beans, cauliflower, peas and a little salt. Cover and cook, stirring occasionally, for 20 minutes or until the vegetables are tender.

3   Remove the pan from the heat and slowly pour in the coconut milk. Stir constantly over a low heat for 2 minutes so that it heats through gently and blends with the other ingredients. Serve immediately.

mixed vegetable masala

This is a far cry from the dreary mixed vegetable curry found on most Indian restaurant menus twenty years ago (and sometimes still today). Combining a wide variety of vegetables is the secret to making this dish a treat for vegetarians and meat-eaters alike. You can use any selection of vegetables – try incorporating tropical varieties such as okra when they are available.

SERVES 4

3 tablespoons vegetable oil

2.5cm (1 inch) piece cinnamon stick

3 cloves

4–5 green cardamom pods, cracked

pinch of fennel seeds

5 shallots, peeled and very finely chopped

4 mixed sweet peppers (red, yellow, orange, green)

4 tomatoes, quartered

3 potatoes, peeled and diced

3 carrots, peeled and diced

100g (3^1/$_2$oz) peas

2 tablespoons chopped coriander leaves, to serve

FOR THE SPICE PASTE:

5 tablespoons yogurt

1 teaspoon tomato purée

1 teaspoon chilli powder

^{1}/$_2$ teaspoon ground cumin

^{1}/$_2$ teaspoon ground turmeric

^{1}/$_2$ teaspoon garam masala

1 To make the spice paste, place the yogurt in a small bowl and stir in the tomato purée, chilli powder, cumin, turmeric and garam masala. Set aside.

2 Heat the oil in a large saucepan. Add the cinnamon, cloves, cardamom pods, fennel seeds and shallots and cook, stirring occasionally, for 10 minutes or until the shallots are soft and golden. Meanwhile, halve, core and deseed the peppers, then cut into dice.

3 Lower the heat under the pan, add the tomatoes and spicy yogurt paste and mix well. Pour in 600ml (1 pint) water and bring the mixture to the boil. Stir in the mixed peppers, potatoes, carrots and peas. Cover and cook for 10–15 minutes or until the vegetables are tender. Remove from the heat and scatter with chopped coriander leaves to serve.

sweet mango pachadi

Pachadi is a popular feast item among Brahmins in South India, probably because its thick, creamy sauce offers a complete contrast to their usual spicy curries, and it can be made using different fruits. During the mango season we would often make this version for family gatherings.

SERVES 4

200g (7oz) ripe mango

25g (1oz) jaggery or palm sugar

2.5cm (1 inch) piece fresh root ginger, peeled and
   finely sliced

1/2 teaspoon ground turmeric

3 tablespoons vegetable oil

1 teaspoon mustard seeds

10 curry leaves

4 dried red chillies

sea salt

FOR THE SPICE PASTE:

75g (3oz) freshly grated coconut

2 green chillies

1 teaspoon mustard powder

1 For the spice paste, place all the ingredients in a blender and add 250ml (8fl oz) water. Process slowly to give a coarse paste.

2 Peel the mango and cut the flesh away from the stone, then cut into 2.5cm (1 inch) cubes. Place in a large saucepan and cover generously with water. Bring to the boil, then lower the heat and simmer for 5 minutes. Add the jaggery, ginger, turmeric and a little salt, and simmer for a further 5 minutes or until the fruit is thoroughly cooked and the jaggery is well blended.

3 Add the coconut spice paste to the pan and stir to combine with the mango mixture, then lower the heat and cook gently for 5 minutes.

4 Just before it is ready, heat the oil in a small frying pan. Add the mustard seeds and, when they start to pop, add the curry leaves and dried chillies and cook for 1 minute. Pour the contents of the pan over the curry, stir to combine, then serve immediately.

moru

No South Indian meal is complete without a yogurt curry known as moru kachiathu, though you might consider it to be more of a sauce than a curry. A thin, smooth and vibrantly yellow mixture of yogurt, ginger and chillies, it seems to enhance the foods it is served with in an almost magical way.

For a light meal, the basic moru can be served simply with cashew and lemon rice (page 166) or appams (pages 158–9). Or for a more substantial curry, vegetables or fruits may be added, the sourness of the yogurt providing a wonderful contrast to sweet fruits – mango and plantain in particular.

When making moru, you must remove the pan from the heat before adding the yogurt, otherwise the mixture will curdle. Blend the yogurt in slowly, stirring all the time. Authentically moru is served lukewarm rather than hot, but it can then be warmed through gently before serving, if you prefer. Each of the following morus serves 4.

▲ spinach and mango moru curry

Heat 1 tbsp oil in a pan. Fry 1 tsp mustard seeds and, when they start to pop, add 1 finely sliced small onion, 20 curry leaves, 2 dried red chillies and 1 tsp salt. Cook for 10 minutes. Add 1 tsp grated ginger and 1 green chilli, slit lengthways. Cook, stirring, for 1 minute. Mix in 1 tsp turmeric, then off the heat slowly stir in 400ml (14fl oz) yogurt. Stir in 25g (1oz) spinach and 1 thinly sliced small mango. Heat gently, stirring, for 1 minute, then serve.

basic moru kachiathu

Heat 1 tbsp oil in a pan and fry 1 tsp mustard seeds until they start to pop. Add 1 finely sliced small onion, 2 dried red chillies, 20 curry leaves and 1 tsp salt. Cook for 10 minutes or until the onion is golden. Add 1 tsp grated ginger and 1 green chilli, slit lengthways. Cook, stirring, for 1 minute. Mix in 1 tsp turmeric, then off the heat slowly stir in 400ml (14fl oz) yogurt. Heat gently for 1 minute, stirring constantly, then serve.

mixed pepper moru curry

Fry 2 tsp mustard seeds in 4 tbsp oil and, as they start to pop, add 3 finely chopped garlic cloves, 3 dried red chillies, ¼ tsp fenugreek seeds and 10 curry leaves. Cook for 2 minutes. Add 2 diced onions, 3 slit green chillies and 1 tbsp finely diced ginger; cook for 10 minutes. Stir in 1 chopped tomato, 1 tsp turmeric and a little salt, then add 150g (5oz) mixed peppers, in strips; cook for 5 minutes. Off the heat, slowly stir in 250g (9oz) yogurt. Heat gently for 1 minute, stirring, then serve.

▲ okra moru curry

Fry 150g (5oz) sliced okra in 2 tbsp oil for 5 minutes until crunchy; drain. Fry 2 tsp mustard seeds in 4 tbsp oil; as they pop add 3 finely chopped garlic cloves, 3 dried red chillies, 10 curry leaves and ¼ tsp fenugreek seeds; cook for 2 minutes. Add 2 diced onions, 3 slit green chillies and 1 tbsp finely diced ginger; cook for 10 minutes. Stir in 1 chopped tomato, 1 tsp turmeric and salt. Add the okra and cook for 5 minutes. Off the heat, slowly stir in 250g (9oz) yogurt. Heat gently, stirring, to serve.

garlic curry

People are always intrigued by this curry and wonder how the strong flavour of garlic is so well tamed by the spicy and tangy tamarind sauce. This is a special recipe given to me by a friend from Karakkudi in Tamil Nadu. It is traditionally eaten with Malabar parathas (page 155).

SERVES 4

75g (3oz) tamarind pulp
3 tablespoons vegetable oil
200g (7oz) garlic cloves, peeled
1 teaspoon fenugreek seeds
2 dried red chillies
1/2 teaspoon fennel seeds

10 curry leaves
3 onions, peeled and finely chopped
3 green chillies, slit lengthways
1/2 teaspoon ground turmeric
1/2 teaspoon chilli powder
2 tomatoes, finely chopped

1 Place the tamarind pulp in a small bowl and add 900ml (1½ pints) hot water. Break up the tamarind pulp as much as possible and set aside to soak for 20–30 minutes. Pass through a sieve into another bowl, pressing to extract as much tamarind flavour from the pulp as possible.

2 Heat 1 tablespoon oil in a frying pan. Add 50g (2oz) garlic, ½ teaspoon fenugreek seeds and the dried chillies and fry for 1 minute. Remove with a slotted spoon and drain on kitchen paper. Transfer the cooked garlic and spices to a blender and process to a fine paste, then set aside.

3 Heat the remaining oil in a large pan. Add the fennel seeds and remaining fenugreek seeds and sauté for 1 minute or until they are brown. Add the curry leaves, onions and chillies. Cook over a medium heat for 5 minutes or until the onions are soft, then add the turmeric and chilli powder, followed by the chopped tomatoes. Mix well and cook for 5 minutes, stirring frequently.

4 Stir in the remaining garlic cloves, the cooked garlic paste and the tamarind liquid. Lower the heat and cook gently, stirring frequently, for 15 minutes or until the mixture is thick and the garlic is well cooked.

green paw paw curry

In Indian cooking, fruit is often used in savoury dishes as though it were a vegetable, and the distinction between fruit and vegetables is somewhat blurred. To achieve the right flavour and texture in this recipe, make sure that the paw paw is green and firm. I love to eat this curry with rice and sweet mango chutney (page 31) for lunch.

SERVES 4

1 firm, unripe paw paw, about 250g (9oz)
3 tablespoons vegetable oil
1 teaspoon mustard seeds
pinch of fenugreek seeds
10 curry leaves, plus extra to garnish
3 dried red chillies
150g (5oz) shallots, peeled and finely chopped
2.5cm (1 inch) piece fresh root ginger, peeled
   and finely sliced
4 green chillies, slit lengthways
250ml (8 fl oz) coconut milk
sea salt

1   Peel and chop the paw paw and place in a large saucepan. Cover generously with water and add a little salt. Bring to the boil, then lower the heat and simmer for 15 minutes or until the paw paw is tender. Drain and set aside.

2   Heat the oil in a large saucepan or wok. Add the mustard seeds and, when they start to pop, add the fenugreek seeds. Sauté for 1 minute or until the seeds just turn golden. Add the curry leaves, dried chillies and shallots and cook for 5 minutes or until the shallots are lightly golden.

3   Add the ginger, green chillies and a pinch of salt. Stir well, then add the cooked paw paw and stir again. Turn the heat right down and slowly add the coconut milk. Remove the pan from the heat and stir the curry constantly for 2 minutes so that the coconut milk heats through gently. Garnish with fresh curry leaves to serve.

courgette curry

Although the courgette is not an Indian vegetable, I was keen to try cooking it with traditional Keralan spices. The refreshing taste of tomatoes with crushed fennel makes this very different from a lot of other curries we offer, and the method of grinding them to a rough paste before cooking is a little unusual too.

SERVES 4

3 tomatoes
2 garlic cloves, peeled
pinch of fennel seeds
3 tablespoons vegetable oil
150g (5oz) shallots or onion, peeled and
  chopped
250g (9oz) courgettes, sliced
1/2 teaspoon ground turmeric
1 teaspoon chilli powder
300ml (1/2 pint) coconut milk

1   Put the tomatoes, garlic cloves and fennel seeds in a blender and process to make a rough paste, then set aside.

2   Heat the oil in a large saucepan, karahi or wok. Add the shallots and cook for 5 minutes or until soft. Add the courgettes, turmeric and chilli powder, and stir-fry for 5 minutes or until the courgettes are cooked but still crunchy.

3   Lower the heat and add the freshly ground tomato paste. Cook, stirring well, for 1 minute, then mix in the coconut milk. Bring to the boil, stirring, then lower the heat and simmer for 5 minutes. Serve hot, with rice or bread.

green pea and pepper curry

I have fond memories of the Cotton Hill canteen in Trivandrum, which I used to visit frequently during my university days. The green pea curry, made with a tomato and onion masala and an abundant dose of cracked black pepper, was so tasty that my mouth begins to water at the very thought of it. You should serve this as they used to, with a Malabar paratha (page 155).

SERVES 4

3 tablespoons vegetable oil

2.5cm (1 inch) piece fresh root ginger, peeled and grated

4 shallots, peeled and finely chopped

2 green chillies, slit lengthways

1 teaspoon ground coriander

1 teaspoon garam masala

1/2 teaspoon ground turmeric

1/2 teaspoon chilli powder

4 tomatoes, finely sliced

300g (11oz) peas

1 red pepper, cored, deseeded and chopped

1 teaspoon cracked black pepper

sea salt

2 tablespoons finely chopped coriander leaves, to serve (optional)

1   Heat the oil in a large frying pan, karahi or wok. Add the grated ginger and sauté for a few seconds, then add the shallots and cook for 5 minutes or until they are soft.

2   Add the chillies, ground coriander, garam masala, turmeric and chilli powder, stir briefly, then add the sliced tomatoes and a little salt. Pour in 100ml (3½fl oz) water and mix well, then cover and cook for 5 minutes until the sauce is thick.

3   Lower the heat and add the peas and red pepper. Cook gently for 10 minutes or until the vegetables are tender. Stir in the cracked black pepper, then scatter with chopped coriander if you like. Serve hot, with parathas.

cauliflower curry

Cauliflower is very popular in North India, and the most typical dish, *aloo gobi*, is found on most restaurant menus. This fresh-tasting curry is best eaten with Malabar parathas (page 155) or cashew and lemon rice (page 166).

SERVES 4

3 tablespoons vegetable oil
1 teaspoon fennel seeds
1 large onion, peeled and finely chopped
$1/2$ teaspoon ground turmeric
$1/2$ teaspoon chilli powder
4 tablespoons tomato purée
250g (9oz) cauliflower florets
150g (5oz) green pepper, cored, deseeded
  and cubed
4 tomatoes, quartered
600ml (1 pint) milk
small bunch of coriander, finely chopped
sea salt

1   Heat the oil in a medium saucepan. Add the fennel seeds and cook, stirring constantly, for 1 minute or until golden brown. Add the onion and cook for 10 minutes, stirring frequently, until golden.

2   Add the turmeric and chilli powder and stir-fry for 2 minutes, then stir in the tomato purée. Add the cauliflower florets, green pepper, tomatoes, milk, 250ml (8fl oz) water and some salt. Cook over a medium heat for 5–8 minutes, stirring constantly to prevent the milk splitting.

3   When the vegetables are tender, scatter with the chopped coriander, toss to mix and serve hot.

broccoli with panch phoron

Every state in India has its own special spice blend that becomes a feature of its cooking and brings a distinctive flavour to the characteristic dishes of the region. Bengal in the North-east is known for its homemade spice powder called panch phoron, which combines equal quantities of five strongly flavoured spices. It is primarily used in vegetarian dishes to enhance flavour and create a pure Bengali aroma. It's easy to make a batch yourself, to keep and use as required.

SERVES 4

3 tablespoons vegetable oil

1 large onion, peeled and sliced

2.5cm (1 inch) piece fresh root ginger, peeled and shredded

2 dried red chillies, chopped

1/2 teaspoon ground turmeric

250g (9oz) broccoli, finely chopped

150g (5oz) white or green cabbage, finely sliced

1 tablespoon ghee

sea salt

FOR THE SPICE POWDER:

2 teaspoons cumin seeds

2 teaspoons fennel seeds

2 teaspoons fenugreek seeds

2 teaspoons mustard seeds

2 teaspoons kalonji (nigella) seeds

1 To make the spice powder, put all the ingredients in a small spice mill and grind to a fine powder. Store in an airtight container.

2 Heat the oil in a large saucepan, karahi or wok. Add the onion and ginger and cook for 10 minutes or until golden. Add the chillies and turmeric, stir well, then add the broccoli, cabbage and a little salt. Sprinkle a few tablespoons of water over the vegetable mixture and cover with a lid. Lower the heat and cook for 10 minutes or until the vegetables are tender.

3 Just before the vegetables are cooked, melt the ghee in a small frying pan. Add 1 teaspoon of the panch phoron spice powder, stir once, then quickly pour the contents of the frying pan over the broccoli mixture. Mix well and serve with chapattis (page 154) or other Indian bread.

pumpkin curry

We grow a variety of pumpkins in South India and for each type there is a particular recipe that best highlights its unique texture and flavour. This recipe is a traditional and colourful feast dish, and the use of roasted coconut really makes it stand out from other dishes on the table. Serve it with a moru curry (page 88) and plain rice.

SERVES 4

400g (14oz) yellow pumpkin
1 teaspoon ground turmeric
1 teaspoon chilli powder
200g (7oz) freshly grated coconut
1/2 teaspoon cumin seeds

3 tablespoons vegetable oil
1 teaspoon mustard seeds
few curry leaves
2 dried red chillies
sea salt

1 Peel, deseed and cube the pumpkin, then place in a saucepan with the turmeric, chilli powder, a little salt and 600ml (1 pint) water. Bring to the boil, then simmer for 5 minutes or until well cooked.

2 Meanwhile, finely grind half of the coconut with the cumin seeds in a spice mill. Stir into the pumpkin mixture and cook for 2 minutes, stirring frequently. Take off the heat.

3 Heat the oil in a frying pan. Add the mustard seeds and, as they start to pop, add the curry leaves, dried chillies and remaining coconut. Cook for about 4 minutes until the coconut is toasted. Tip the coconut mixture over the pumpkin curry, stir and serve.

sweet potato curry

A curry made from sweet potato is something unusual. Care must be taken to balance the spices with the sweetness of the vegetable, so follow the quantities precisely.

SERVES 4

400g (14oz) sweet potatoes, peeled and diced
3 green chillies
2.5cm (1 inch) piece fresh root ginger, peeled and
   thinly sliced

200ml (7fl oz) coconut milk
10 curry leaves
sea salt

1 Put the sweet potatoes in a large saucepan with the chillies and ginger. Add just enough water to cover and a pinch of salt. Bring to the boil, then simmer, stirring occasionally, for 10 minutes or until the potatoes are tender.

2 Lower the heat and stir in the coconut milk and curry leaves. Simmer gently, stirring, for a few minutes to heat through, then serve.

5 fish and shellfish

marinated sardines

Fish dishes are hugely popular in India's coastal states and this recipe is typical of Cochin and other backwater areas, where it is eaten for lunch. You only have to walk around the town to savour its tempting aroma, because so many people will be cooking it. Although sardines work particularly well cooked in this way, you can use other oily fish too.

SERVES 2–3

450g (1lb) sardines, cleaned

4 tablespoons vegetable oil

FOR THE SPICE PASTE:

2 tablespoons lemon juice

2.5cm (1 inch) piece fresh root ginger, peeled
and chopped

4 garlic cloves, peeled and crushed

1 teaspoon chilli powder

large pinch of ground turmeric

sea salt

TO SERVE:

lime wedges

1   First make the spice paste. Grind the lemon juice, ginger, garlic, chilli powder, turmeric and a little salt together to a fine paste, using a pestle and mortar or a small blender goblet.

2   Using a sharp knife, slash the sardines diagonally on both sides to allow the flavourings to permeate the flesh. Lay them side by side in a non-metallic dish, rub the spice paste all over and set aside to marinate for 10 minutes.

3   Heat the oil in a large frying pan and cook the sardines in batches if necessary. Place in a single layer in the pan and fry over a low heat for about 2–3 minutes on each side until brown and crispy. Serve hot, with lime wedges.

tuna and potato cutlets

Tuna cutlets are often sold as a snack in Indian bakeries. Serve these with a fresh chutney, or garlic and chilli pickle (page 27). Shaped into smaller patties, they make a good party snack.

MAKES 6–8
275g (10oz) tuna steaks, cubed
275g (10oz) potato, peeled and cubed
1/2 teaspoon ground turmeric, plus a pinch
2 tablespoons vegetable oil
1 teaspoon mustard seeds
10 curry leaves
2.5cm (1 inch) piece fresh root ginger, peeled and chopped

1 green chilli, chopped
2 onions, peeled and chopped
1/2 teaspoon chilli powder
1 teaspoon garam masala
150g (5oz) cornflour
113g pack natural dried breadcrumbs
vegetable oil, for deep-frying
sea salt

1 Put the tuna, potato cubes, 1/2 teaspoon turmeric and a little salt in a saucepan. Add enough water to just cover and simmer until the potato is just cooked, about 15 minutes. Drain and transfer to a bowl.

2 Heat 2 tablespoons oil in a large frying pan. Add the mustard seeds and, as they start to pop, add the curry leaves, ginger, chilli and onions and sauté for 5 minutes or until the onions are soft. Add the chilli powder, garam masala and pinch of turmeric. Cook gently for 2 minutes, stirring. Add to the tuna and potato and mash the mixture. Leave until cool enough to handle.

3 Divide the tuna mixture into 6–8 equal portions then, using wet hands, form into teardrop-shaped cutlets. Blend the cornflour with 200ml (7fl oz) water. Spread the breadcrumbs on a baking tray. Heat the oil for deep-frying in a suitable pan to 180°–190°C.

4 Dip each cutlet into the cornflour liquid, then coat with the breadcrumbs, pressing them on gently. Deep-fry in batches for 3–5 minutes until golden, turning frequently. Drain on kitchen paper and serve.

fish steamed in banana leaves

This dish is renowned in Kerala, where steamed fish, known as *meen elayil pollichathu*, are popular. Steaming allows you to enjoy the full flavour of the fish, and banana leaves add a special essence to the final dish. If you cannot find banana leaves, foil is a good alternative.
Illustrated on previous page

SERVES 2–4

2 mackerel, each about 350g (12oz), cleaned
  and cut into 2.5cm (1 inch) slices
1 large banana leaf

FOR THE SPICE PASTE:
100g (3½oz) coriander leaves, chopped
1 onion, peeled and chopped
3 garlic cloves, peeled and chopped
1cm (½ inch) piece fresh root ginger, peeled
  and chopped
1 green chilli, chopped
½ teaspoon ground black pepper
2 tablespoons lime juice
sea salt

1   To make the spice paste, place the chopped coriander, onion, garlic, ginger, chilli, black pepper and lime juice in a blender. Add a little salt and process to a smooth paste.

2   Transfer the spice paste to a large bowl, add the fish pieces and rub the paste carefully into the flesh. Set aside to marinate for 10 minutes.

3   Position a large steamer over a pan of water and bring to the boil. Dip the banana leaf briefly in a dish of hot water to soften and make it pliable, then shake gently to remove excess water and spread it out on a work surface.

4   Place the fish on the banana leaf, re-assembling it if you like, and spread the excess spice paste on top of the fish. Carefully wrap the leaf around the filling to make a parcel. Secure with string, strips of banana leaf, or small skewers. Place the parcel in the steamer and cook for 5–6 minutes.

5   To serve, lift the banana-wrapped fish on to a hot platter. Unwrap the parcel at the table so that everyone can savour the aroma.

lemon sole in tamarind sauce

This spicy, red-coloured dish has an unforgettable and distinctive flavour thanks to the use of tamarind. In India, it would be cooked in a terracotta pot over a slow fire. Although I'm using lemon sole here, any similar white fish can be substituted.

SERVES 6

50g (2oz) tamarind pulp

2 tablespoons vegetable oil

1 teaspoon mustard seeds

10 curry leaves

pinch of fenugreek seeds

2 onions, peeled and chopped

$1/4$ teaspoon ground turmeric

$1/2$ teaspoon chilli powder

1 teaspoon ground coriander

3 tomatoes, chopped

1 teaspoon tomato purée

600g (1$1/4$lb) lemon sole fillets

sea salt

1 Place the tamarind pulp in a small heatproof bowl and break it up as much as possible. Add 100ml (3$1/2$fl oz) hot water and set aside to soak for 20 minutes. Press the mixture through a sieve into a bowl and set aside, discarding the residue in the sieve.

2 Meanwhile, heat the oil in a large saucepan, karahi or wok. Add the mustard seeds and, when they start to pop, add the curry leaves and fenugreek seeds. Sauté for 1–2 minutes or until the fenugreek seeds turn brown. Stir in the onions and cook over a medium heat, stirring occasionally, for 10 minutes or until they are golden.

3 Add the turmeric, chilli powder and ground coriander, mix well, then add the chopped tomatoes, tomato purée and a little salt and cook for a further 2 minutes. Pour in the tamarind liquid and 200ml (7fl oz) water. Bring the mixture to the boil and simmer for 10–12 minutes, stirring occasionally, until the sauce thickens.

4 Cut the fish fillets into 2.5cm (1 inch) pieces and carefully mix into the sauce. Lower the heat and cook gently for 4–5 minutes or until the fish is just cooked through. Remove the pan from the heat and serve immediately.

lemon sole with coconut

The use of coconut milk in fish curries is typical of the inland areas of Kerala. Its smooth, creamy taste provides a soothing quality that appeals to those who prefer mild curries, and it certainly makes the dish look appetising. Other white fish can be used instead of lemon sole, if you prefer.

SERVES 6

2 tablespoons vegetable oil
200g (7oz) shallots, peeled and chopped
10 curry leaves
600g (1¼ lb) lemon sole fillets

FOR THE SPICE PASTE:
100g (3½oz) freshly grated coconut
1 teaspoon ground coriander
½ teaspoon chilli powder
large pinch of ground turmeric

1 To make the spice paste, place the coconut, ground coriander, chilli powder and turmeric in a blender. Pour in 200ml (7 fl oz) water and process for 2–3 minutes to a smooth paste. Set aside.

2 Heat the oil in a large frying pan, karahi or wok. Add the shallots and curry leaves and cook over a medium-low heat for 5 minutes or until the shallots are soft. Stir in the coconut spice paste together with 100ml (3½ fl oz) water and bring the mixture to the boil. Cook for about 5 minutes, stirring occasionally, until the sauce thickens.

3 Cut the fish fillets into 2.5cm (1 inch) pieces, add to the sauce and mix carefully. Cook gently for 4–5 minutes or until the fish is cooked through. Remove the pan from the heat and serve immediately.

salmon curry

This fish curry is popular in toddy shops (local village bars) across India, and so famously delicious that even teetotallers visit regularly to enjoy it. Here I am using salmon, but of course in India it would be prepared with the local catch. Accompany with rice or potatoes.

SERVES 4–6

1 tablespoon tamarind pulp

2 tablespoons vegetable oil

1/2 teaspoon mustard seeds

10 curry leaves

pinch of fenugreek seeds

1 large onion, peeled and chopped

1/2 teaspoon ground turmeric

1/2 teaspoon chilli powder

1 teaspoon ground coriander

2 tomatoes, chopped

500g (1lb 2oz) salmon fillet, cubed

200ml (7 fl oz) coconut milk

sea salt

1 Place the tamarind pulp in a small heatproof bowl and cover with 3 tablespoons hot water. Use a teaspoon to break up the tamarind as much as possible, then set aside to soften for 15–20 minutes. Push the mixture through a sieve to extract 3 tablespoons of tamarind-flavoured liquid, discarding any seeds and fibres.

2 Meanwhile, heat the oil in a large saucepan, karahi or wok. Add the mustard seeds and, when they start to pop, add the curry leaves and fenugreek seeds. Fry for 1 minute or until golden. Add the onion and cook over a medium-low heat for 10 minutes, stirring occasionally, until golden.

3 Add the turmeric, chilli powder and ground coriander and cook for a further minute. Add the tomatoes and a little salt and cook for 2 minutes, stirring constantly. Pour in the tamarind liquid and 300ml (1/2 pint) water and slowly bring to the boil.

4 Meanwhile, cut the salmon into 4cm (11/2 inch) pieces. Lower the heat under the pan, add the fish cubes and simmer for 5–6 minutes or until the salmon is just cooked through.

5 Turn the heat as low as possible and pour in the coconut milk. Simmer gently for 2 minutes, then remove the pan from the heat and serve immediately.

fried fish Indian style

Here is India's spicy take on fish and chips. Fried fish in batter is often made at home on the subcontinent, but more importantly, it's a favourite snack sold in India's popular *thattukada* or street refreshment places.

The secret of successful deep-frying is to make sure that the oil is at the correct temperature before the batter-coated fish is added. The oil should register 180–190°C on a thermometer, or you can test by adding a cube of bread – this should brown in 30 seconds. It is also important that the pan is not overcrowded, because this will lower the temperature of the oil. Add the coated pieces of fish one or two at a time.

In India, fried battered fish is generally eaten plain, but I've suggested suitable chutneys to accompany if you prefer. These batter recipes are enough to coat 450g (1lb) fish or seafood, which will serve 4. Experiment with different fish and shellfish according to availability.

▲ **spiced batter**
In a blender, mix 100g (3½oz) chick pea flour with 50g (2oz) rice flour, 4 tbsp chopped coriander leaves, 1 chopped green chilli, 1 tsp chilli powder, ½ tsp garam masala, a pinch of turmeric and a little salt. Slowly blend in 200ml (7fl oz) water to make a smooth batter. Cut 450g (1lb) fish fillets into strips, dip in the batter, then deep-fry in hot oil for 1 minute until golden. Serve with sweet mango chutney (page 31).

hot pepper batter

Mix 200g (7oz) plain flour, ½ tsp baking powder, 1 tsp crushed black pepper, pinch of salt, 1 tsp chilli powder and ¼ tsp ground turmeric in a bowl and make a well. Whisk 4 eggs with 90ml (3fl oz) milk, then pour into the well and gradually mix to a smooth, thick batter. Rest for 20 minutes. Cut 450g (1lb) fish fillets into strips, dip in the batter, then deep-fry in hot oil for 1 minute until golden. Serve plain or with a chutney.

▲ spiced coconut milk batter

Put 150g (5oz) cornflour in a bowl with 3 finely chopped garlic cloves, 2.5cm (1 inch) piece finely chopped fresh root ginger, 10 chopped curry leaves, 1 tsp chilli powder, ¼ tsp turmeric and a little salt. Make a well in the centre and add 1 beaten egg, then 100ml (3½fl oz) coconut milk. Mix to a smooth, thick batter. Cut 450g (1lb) fish fillets into strips, dip in the batter, then deep-fry in hot oil for 1 minute until golden. Serve plain or with sweet mango chutney (page 31).

▲ spinach and curry leaf batter

In a blender, mix 100g (3½oz) chick pea flour with 50g (2oz) rice flour, 50g (2oz) finely chopped spinach leaves, 20 finely chopped curry leaves, 1 chopped green chilli, 1 tsp chilli powder, ½ tsp garam masala, a pinch of turmeric and a little salt. Slowly blend in 200ml (7fl oz) water to make a smooth batter. Peel 450g (1lb) raw king prawns, leaving the tails on. Dip into the batter, then deep-fry in the hot oil for 1–2 minutes until crisp and golden. Serve with coconut chutney (page 30).

prawn stir-fry

Rahul Dravid, one of India's most famous cricketers, came to our restaurant last year and asked us to make him a crunchy shrimp or prawn dish with plenty of curry leaves and onions. He even told me how his mum would make it for him during his occasional visits back home. Our attempt wasn't bad … Rahul liked it so much he returned four times. It is easy to make at home, and full of crunchy fresh flavours.

SERVES 4

*400g (14oz) prawns (preferably raw),
  peeled*
vegetable oil, for deep-frying
2 tablespoons vegetable oil
1/2 teaspoon mustard seeds
10 curry leaves
100g (3 1/2 oz) shallots, peeled and sliced
1/2 teaspoon ground turmeric
1/2 teaspoon chilli powder
1 green chilli, slit lengthways
1 tablespoon lemon juice
1/2 teaspoon ground black pepper
sea salt

1 Cut the prawns into 1cm (1/2 inch) pieces. Heat the oil for deep-frying in a large, heavy-based saucepan, karahi or wok to 180°–190°C or until a cube of bread browns in 30 seconds. Add the prawns and deep-fry until lightly golden; allow 45 seconds for cooked prawns; 1 1/2 minutes for raw. Remove with a slotted spoon and set aside to drain on kitchen paper.

2 Heat 2 tablespoons oil in a large frying pan, karahi or wok. Add the mustard seeds and, when they start to pop, add the curry leaves and shallots. Cook, stirring, for 5 minutes or until the shallots are soft. Stir in the turmeric, chilli powder, green chilli and some salt. Cook, stirring, for a further 2 minutes.

3 Add the prawns and stir-fry over a medium-low heat for 5 minutes. Pour in the lemon juice, then stir in the black pepper, remove the pan from the heat and serve immediately.

prawns with toasted coconut sauce

We are following in the footsteps of an old Hindu dish with this recipe. The toasted coconut spice paste is often used in vegetable dishes too. We serve this popular dish with adipoli parathas (page 156); add a side dish of thoran (pages 42–3) and you will have an excellent meal.

SERVES 4–6

3 tablespoons vegetable oil

1/2 teaspoon mustard seeds

10 curry leaves

1 large onion, peeled and chopped

1/2 teaspoon ground turmeric

1/2 teaspoon chilli powder

2 tomatoes, quartered

500g (1lb 2oz) raw prawns, peeled

50ml (2 fl oz) coconut milk

2 tablespoons lime juice

sea salt

FOR THE SPICE PASTE:

2 tablespoons coriander seeds

100g (3 1/2 oz) freshly grated coconut

10 curry leaves

1 dried red chilli

1   To make the spice paste, place all the ingredients in a dry frying pan and toast over a medium-low heat, stirring constantly, for 5 minutes or until the coconut turns brown. Set aside to cool.

2   Transfer the toasted coconut mixture to a blender or food processor and process, gradually adding 300ml (1/2 pint) water to make a thin, smooth paste. Set aside.

3   Heat the oil in a large saucepan, karahi or wok. Add the mustard seeds and, when they start to pop, add the curry leaves and onion. Cook for 10 minutes, stirring occasionally, until the onion is light golden. Add the turmeric, chilli powder, tomatoes and a little salt and cook, stirring, for 2 minutes.

4   Pour in the coconut paste, then increase the heat and bring the mixture to the boil. Add the prawns and simmer for 5 minutes or until they turn pink and are cooked. Lower the heat, stir in the coconut milk and simmer gently for 2 minutes. Remove the pan from the heat, stir in the lime juice and serve.

prawn and mango curry

In India, prawns are very expensive and considered a luxury food. Consequently, a king prawn curry is something enjoyed only on special occasions, or when prawns are sold cheaply in the market. Serve this light, mild dish with a rice dish or appams (pages 158–9).

SERVES 4–6

2 tablespoons vegetable oil

$^1/_2$ teaspoon mustard seeds

10 curry leaves

2.5cm (1 inch) piece fresh root ginger, peeled
   and cut into julienne strips

2 green chillies, slit lengthways

2 large onions, peeled and sliced

1 unripened mango, peeled, stoned and cubed

$^1/_2$ teaspoon ground turmeric

400ml (14 fl oz) coconut milk

500g (1lb 2oz) raw king prawns, peeled
   with tails left on

sea salt

1 Heat the oil in a large frying pan, karahi or wok. Add the mustard seeds and, when they start to pop, add the curry leaves, ginger, chillies and onions. Cook over a medium-low heat for 10 minutes, stirring occasionally, until the onions are golden.

2 Add the mango, turmeric and a little salt and mix well for 1 minute, then pour in the coconut milk and 200ml (7 fl oz) water. Bring the mixture to the boil, stirring constantly.

3 Add the prawns to the pan and cook, stirring, for 5–6 minutes or until they turn pink and are cooked. Serve immediately, with rice or appams.

prawn and tomato curry

This authentic Keralan recipe originates from Koyilandi near Calicut in the north of the state. It has a thick consistency, making it a good alternative to the more usual saucy dishes. For a complete meal, serve it with adipoli parathas (page 156) and a dish of spicy new potatoes with spinach (page 53). Alternatively, serve the curry on lightly toasted poppadoms.

SERVES 4–6

3 tablespoons vegetable oil
pinch of cumin seeds
10 curry leaves
3 onions, peeled and sliced
1/2 teaspoon ground turmeric
1 teaspoon chilli powder
1 teaspoon tomato purée
4 tomatoes, sliced
500g (1lb 2oz) raw king prawns, peeled
   with tails left on
sea salt
chopped coriander leaves, to serve

1   Heat the oil in a large frying pan, karahi or wok. Add the cumin seeds, curry leaves and onions and cook over a medium-low heat for 10 minutes, stirring occasionally, until the onions are golden.

2   Add the turmeric, chilli powder, tomato purée, tomatoes and a little salt. Cook for 5 minutes, stirring constantly.

3   Add the prawns and cook for a further 5–6 minutes or until they turn pink and are cooked through. Serve scattered with chopped coriander leaves.

pepper-fried crab

If you want to eat crab, this is the way to do it: make a mess with the shell and thoroughly enjoy it. Some people complain about the difficulty of extracting the meat from the shell, but it is well worth the effort. People keep telling me this is the best crab dish they have ever tasted.

SERVES 2–4

1 medium cooked crab, about 450g (1lb), cleaned

2 tablespoons ghee

1cm (½ inch) piece fresh root ginger, peeled and crushed

2 garlic cloves, peeled and crushed

10 curry leaves

1 large red onion, peeled and sliced

½ teaspoon ground turmeric

1 green chilli, finely sliced

2 tomatoes, cut into wedges

3 tablespoons lemon juice

1 teaspoon ground black pepper

sea salt

1 Using a strong knife, halve or quarter the crab. Make sure that the small stomach sac behind the mouth and the inedible, feathery grey gills ('dead man's fingers') are removed.

2 Heat the ghee in a large frying pan, karahi or wok. Add the ginger, garlic, curry leaves and red onion and stir-fry over a medium-low heat for 3 minutes.

3 Add the turmeric, chopped chilli, tomato wedges and some salt to the pan and continue stir-frying for a further 2 minutes.

4 Increase the heat slightly, then add the crab pieces and stir-fry for 2 minutes. Lower the heat, add the lemon juice and black pepper and cook gently for a further 3 minutes. Serve immediately.

crab thoran

Fresh coconut gives this simple recipe a lovely light texture. It is a dry dish that can be eaten on its own or as a side dish. Here it is made with white crabmeat, but it also works well with prawns.

SERVES 4

2 tablespoons vegetable oil
1/2 teaspoon mustard seeds
10 curry leaves
3 garlic cloves, peeled and chopped
2.5cm (1 inch) piece fresh root ginger, peeled
  and finely chopped
2 large onions, peeled and chopped
150g (5oz) coconut, freshly grated
1/2 teaspoon ground turmeric
1/2 teaspoon chilli powder
1/2 teaspoon ground black pepper
400g (14oz) cooked white crabmeat
sea salt

1 Heat the oil in a large frying pan, karahi or wok. Add the mustard seeds and, when they start to pop, add the curry leaves, garlic, ginger and onions. Cook over a medium-low heat, stirring occasionally, for 5 minutes or until the onions are soft.

2 Add the grated coconut, turmeric, chilli powder, black pepper and a little salt and stir-fry for 2 minutes. Increase the heat slightly, then add the crabmeat and continue stir-frying for a further 4–5 minutes. Serve at once.

curried mussels

When I visited Beppoor Port in the north of Kerala during a spice trail trip last year, we came across mussel dishes in almost every restaurant. This is thanks to Arabic trade in the area centuries ago, when Kerala was a regular stop on the way to Sri Lanka. Beppoor Port boasts many mussel dishes including spicy stir-fries, steamed rice dishes, and mussels in coconut sauce. My guests found this one most simple and tasty.

SERVES 2–4

450g (1lb) fresh mussels
2 tablespoons vegetable oil
1/2 teaspoon cumin seeds
1 bay leaf
5 garlic cloves, peeled and finely chopped
2 onions, peeled and finely chopped
1/2 teaspoon ground turmeric, plus a large pinch
2 tomatoes, finely chopped
2 tablespoons lime juice
2 tablespoons chopped coriander leaves
sea salt

1 Clean the mussels by scrubbing the shells under cold running water and removing any beards that are attached to them. Discard any with cracked or broken shells, or any that refuse to close when tapped sharply with a knife. Set the prepared mussels aside.

2 Heat the oil in a large frying pan. Add the cumin seeds, bay leaf, garlic and onions and fry for about 5 minutes until the onions are soft. Add 1/2 teaspoon turmeric, a pinch of salt and the tomatoes. Cook over a low heat, stirring well, for 3 minutes.

3 Meanwhile, put the mussels in a large saucepan with a large pinch of turmeric and a little salt. Add cold water to cover and bring to the boil. Simmer for 2–3 minutes or until the mussels have steamed opened. Discard any that do not open.

4 Quickly drain the mussels, reserving the cooking liquid. Add the mussels to the onion mixture and cook, stirring, for 2 minutes. If you would like the sauce to be thinner, add some of the reserved mussel cooking water. Add the lime juice and scatter in the chopped coriander leaves. Remove the pan from the heat and serve immediately.

6 poultry and meat

marinated chicken with hot pepper sauce

The Andhra Pradesh region is well known for its fiery dishes that use a variety of chillies. People there believe that chilli was the first thing grown in the world and that it should be the main ingredient of any dish – you can imagine how hot the food can get! Not everyone can handle chillies in the same way, however and, after a point, adding more chilli to a dish does not necessarily make it taste better in my opinion, so here is a moderately fiery version.

SERVES 4

4 chicken portions (quarters or breasts)
4 garlic cloves, peeled and chopped
2.5cm (1 inch) piece fresh root ginger, peeled and sliced
3 tablespoons vegetable oil
10 curry leaves
2 onions, peeled and finely chopped
2 teaspoons ground coriander
$1/2$ teaspoon chilli powder
$1/2$ teaspoon ground turmeric
2 tomatoes, chopped
1 teaspoon ground black pepper

FOR THE SPICE PASTE:

1 teaspoon garam masala
$1/2$ teaspoon ground turmeric
sea salt

1   To make the spice paste, mix the garam masala, turmeric and a little salt with about 2 tablespoons water in a small bowl. Place the chicken portions in a shallow, non-metallic dish and spread the paste all over them. Set aside to marinate for 10 minutes.

2   Meanwhile, using a mortar and pestle or small spice mill, grind the garlic and ginger together to make a paste. Set aside.

3   Heat the oil in a saucepan, karahi or wok. Add the curry leaves and onions and fry for 2 minutes, then add the garlic-ginger paste and cook, stirring occasionally, for 5 minutes or until the onions are soft. Add the ground coriander, chilli powder and turmeric, stir well, then add the tomatoes and a little salt. Cook gently for 1–2 minutes.

4   Lay the marinated chicken portions in the pan, spooning some of the onion mixture over the top. Pour in 600ml (1 pint) water and bring to a simmer. Cook for 20–25 minutes or until the chicken is cooked through. Stir in the black pepper, cook for a further 2 minutes, then serve hot.

chicken with roasted coconut

There is nothing quite like the wonderful aroma of freshly roasted coconut. The ingredients in this recipe are beautifully balanced and the resulting dish has a lovely colour and natural creamy coconut flavour.

SERVES 4

500g (1lb 2oz) skinless chicken thigh fillets
3 tablespoons vegetable oil
1/2 teaspoon mustard seeds
10 curry leaves
2 onions, peeled and finely sliced
2 tomatoes, chopped
1/2 teaspoon ground turmeric
sea salt

FOR THE SPICE PASTE:
1 tablespoon vegetable oil
100g (31/2oz) freshly grated coconut
2 bay leaves
1 cinnamon stick
1/2 teaspoon ground black pepper
2 cloves
1 teaspoon ground coriander
1/2 teaspoon chilli powder

1   To make the spice paste, heat the oil in a frying pan. Add the coconut, bay leaves, cinnamon stick, black pepper and cloves and toast, stirring constantly, for 3–5 minutes or until the coconut is golden.

2   Take off the heat and stir in the ground coriander and chilli powder. Discard the cinnamon stick. Tip into a blender, pour in 400ml (14fl oz) water and process for 3–5 minutes to a fine paste. Set aside.

3   Cut the chicken into thick strips and set aside. Heat 3 tablespoons oil in a large saucepan, karahi or wok. Add the mustard seeds and, when they start to pop, add the curry leaves and onions. Cook, stirring frequently, for 5 minutes or until the onions are soft.

4   Add the tomatoes, turmeric and a little salt and stir-fry for 2 minutes. Add the chicken, coconut paste and 600ml (1 pint) water and bring to a simmer. Cook gently for 15–20 minutes or until the chicken is cooked through. Serve hot.

home-style chicken

Known as *kozhy curry*, this dish is often made at home in India. It is quick and simple, and uses ingredients that are easy to find – an ideal recipe for those who have little time to cook. Boneless chicken thighs are convenient, but using chicken on the bone will give the sauce a richer flavour. *Illustrated on previous page*

SERVES 4

3 tablespoons vegetable oil
2.5cm (1 inch) piece cinnamon stick
2 bay leaves
3 cloves
2 onions, peeled and chopped
10 curry leaves
1 tablespoon ground coriander
1 teaspoon garam masala
1/2 teaspoon ground turmeric
1/2 teaspoon chilli powder
2 tomatoes, finely chopped
500g (1lb 2oz) skinless chicken thighs fillets,
   cubed, or 750g (1lb 10oz) chicken pieces
   on the bone
sea salt
2 tablespoons chopped coriander leaves, to serve

1 Heat the oil in a large saucepan or flameproof casserole. Add the cinnamon stick, bay leaves and cloves and cook for 1–2 minutes or until fragrant. Add the onions and curry leaves and cook, stirring occasionally, for 5 minutes or until the onions are soft.

2 Stir in the ground coriander, garam masala, turmeric and chilli powder, then stir in the tomatoes and a little salt. Cook for 5 minutes, stirring occasionally.

3 Add the chicken, mix well, then pour in 350ml (12fl oz) water. Bring to a simmer and cook gently for 15 minutes or until the chicken is cooked through. Serve scattered with the coriander leaves.

Bengali chicken curry

This recipe was given to me by a friend from Calcutta, an ancient and fascinating city. When I expressed my interest in the Bengalis' unique style of cooking, she gave me several recipes and this simple chicken dish was my favourite.

SERVES 4–6

500g (1lb 2oz) skinless chicken thigh or breast
   fillets, cubed
1/4 teaspoon ground turmeric
4 tablespoons vegetable oil
sea salt
3 tablespoons coriander leaves, finely chopped,
   to serve

FOR THE SPICE PASTE:

6 shallots, peeled and chopped
2 green chillies, chopped
3 garlic cloves, peeled
2.5cm (1 inch) piece fresh root ginger, peeled
   and chopped
1 teaspoon ground mustard seeds
1/2 teaspoon ground turmeric

1 For the spice paste, place all the ingredients in a blender and process, adding a few tablespoons of water to make a smooth, thick paste.

2 Place the chicken in a non-metallic bowl. In another bowl, mix together the turmeric, a pinch of salt and a tiny amount of water to make a smooth paste. Rub this mixture all over the chicken and set aside for 5–10 minutes or so.

3 Heat 2 tablespoons oil in a large frying pan or wok. Add the chicken and stir-fry over a medium heat for 10 minutes or until it is golden. Remove the pan from the heat and set aside.

4 Heat the remaining oil in another large saucepan. Add the spice paste and fry over a low heat for 2 minutes, then add the chicken and cook gently, stirring well, for 3–4 minutes. Pour in 300ml (1/2 pint) water, cover the pan and simmer gently over a medium heat for 15 minutes or until the chicken is cooked through. Scatter with chopped coriander leaves and serve hot.

duck curry

Duck is not a typical ingredient for most Indian people, but in Kerala, our beautiful backwater region has lots of ducks and several Christian dishes feature them. Goa and Mangalore, too, have some interesting duck curries.

SERVES 4–6

5 tablespoons vegetable oil
1/4 teaspoon fennel seeds
pinch of fenugreek seeds
2 large onions, peeled and sliced
2 green chillies, chopped
2.5cm (1 inch) piece fresh root ginger, peeled and finely shredded
1 teaspoon ground turmeric
1/2 teaspoon chilli powder
450g (1lb) duck breast, cubed
200g (7oz) baby new potatoes, halved if large
5 tablespoons wine or cider vinegar
400ml (14fl oz) coconut milk
few curry leaves, or to taste
sea salt

1   Heat the oil in a large saucepan. Add the fennel and fenugreek seeds and stir-fry for 30 seconds. Add the onions, chillies and ginger to the pan and fry over a medium heat for 5 minutes or until the onions are soft.

2   Sprinkle in the turmeric, chilli powder and a little salt. Mix well, then add the duck and potatoes, stir well and stir-fry for 10 minutes or until lightly browned.

3   Pour in the vinegar, then stir in 200ml (7fl oz) coconut milk and 250ml (8fl oz) water. Lower the heat to medium-low, cover and cook gently for 20 minutes, stirring occasionally.

4   When the duck is tender and the potatoes are well cooked, turn the heat right down and pour in the remaining 200ml (7fl oz) coconut milk, stirring to combine. Gently mix in the curry leaves, then remove the pan from the heat and serve the curry hot.

tikka

The marinated and grilled dishes known as tikka originated in India's north-west and can be traced further back to Iran and its Persian cooking. In fact, ovens similar to the Indian tandoor can be found in many parts of central and near Asia. It is not possible to reproduce their intense, dry heat in the home kitchen, however grilling and frying tikka foods still produces delicious results.

In recent years tikka dishes seem to have caught the British imagination, no doubt because it is a light and healthy way of enjoying spicy food. Chicken tikka seems to appear everywhere – even as a filling for sandwiches and wraps!

Chicken tikka masala is said to be the world's most popular Indian dish, yet it originated in English curry houses. This 'marinated and grilled chicken in a creamy tomato sauce' appears in many guises. We have our own version and hope you like it! Each of the following tikka recipes serves 4.

▲ lamb tikka with naan
Rub the tikka marinade thickly and evenly over 500g (1lb 2oz) cubed lamb. Marinate for 15–20 minutes, then thread on to 4 metal skewers. Heat 4 tbsp oil in a pan. Add the kebabs and cook, turning, for 10 minutes until brown and crunchy on all sides. Meanwhile, sprinkle 4 naan breads with water and bake according to pack instructions. Serve the tikka with the naan, lime wedges, a tomato, cucumber and onion salad and coconut or sweet mango chutney (page 31).

chicken or duck tikka

Rub the tikka marinade thickly and evenly over 500g (1lb 2 oz) cubed chicken or duck breast fillets and marinate in a non-metallic dish for 15–20 minutes. Thread the meat on to 4 metal skewers or pre-soaked wooden skewers. Grill or barbecue for 5–10 minutes, turning frequently, until browned on all sides. You can also cook salmon and thick white fish fillets, such as halibut, in this way.

▼ chicken tikka masala

Rub the tikka marinade thickly and evenly over 500g (1lb 2oz) cubed chicken breast fillets and leave to marinate for 15–20 minutes. Heat 4 tbsp vegetable oil in a pan and sauté 1 large chopped onion for 10 minutes until soft. Grind 4 garlic cloves and 2.5cm (1 inch) finely chopped ginger together to make a paste, add this to the pan and sauté for 2 minutes. Stir in ½ tsp ground turmeric, ½ tsp chilli powder and 1 tsp ground

▲ tikka marinade

Using a mortar and pestle, grind 2.5cm (1 inch) chopped fresh ginger with 3 garlic cloves to make a smooth paste. Place in a bowl and add 225g (8oz) yogurt, 1 tbsp lime juice, 1 tbsp chopped coriander leaves, ½ tsp chilli powder, ¼ tsp ground turmeric, a large pinch of garam masala and sea salt to taste. Whisk together until smooth, then use to marinate your chosen ingredients.

coriander. Add 1 tsp tomato purée, 200g (7oz) chopped tomatoes and 1 chopped green pepper; sauté for 2 minutes. Pour in 350ml (12 fl oz) water, bring to the boil and cook, covered, for 20–25 minutes. Grill the chicken until lightly charred. When the sauce is thick, lower the heat and pour in 4 tbsp double cream. Add the grilled chicken and salt to taste. Heat through for a few minutes. Serve sprinkled with ¼ tsp garam masala and 2 tbsp chopped coriander leaves.

pork vindaloo

Vindaloo is a very traditional preparation from Goa, the famous tourist paradise. Pork dishes are not common elsewhere in India, but Goan cuisine has a strong Portuguese influence and the population is predominately Christian, so meat is used liberally. Locals love vindaloo's intense spicy flavour, which provides a good contrast to their milder, creamier coconut dishes. The traditional method is time-consuming and labour-intensive, so here is a modified version. Use beef, lamb, chicken or prawns, if you prefer.

SERVES 6–8

900g (2 lb) boneless pork, cubed
4 tablespoons vegetable oil
3 garlic cloves, peeled and chopped
2 onions, peeled and sliced
1 teaspoon ground turmeric
1/2 teaspoon chilli powder
1 teaspoon tomato purée
3 tomatoes, chopped
3 tablespoons wine or cider vinegar
sea salt
coriander leaves, to serve

FOR THE SPICE PASTE:

1 teaspoon cumin seeds
4 dried red chillies
4 cardamom pods
4 cloves
2.5cm (1 inch) piece cinnamon stick
10 black peppercorns
2.5cm (1 inch) piece fresh root ginger, peeled and chopped
4 garlic cloves, peeled
3 tablespoons wine or cider vinegar

1   To make the spice paste, put the cumin seeds, dried chillies, cardamom pods, cloves, cinnamon and peppercorns in a small spice mill and grind to a fine powder. Transfer to a blender and add the ginger and the garlic. Add the vinegar and process to a smooth paste.

2   Place the pork in a large, non-metallic bowl, add the spice paste and stir to coat well. Cover with cling film and set aside to marinate in a cool place for 1 1/2 hours.

3   Heat the oil in a large saucepan or flameproof casserole. Add the garlic and sauté for 1 minute. Add the onions and cook gently for 10–15 minutes, stirring occasionally, until the onions are golden.

4   Add the turmeric, chilli powder, tomato purée, chopped tomatoes and 3 tablespoons vinegar. Mix well, then add the marinated pork and a little salt and cook, stirring constantly, for 10 minutes.

5   Pour in 275ml (9 fl oz) water and bring the mixture to the boil. Lower the heat, cover and simmer gently for 30 minutes or until the meat is cooked through and the sauce is thick. Serve hot, scattered with coriander leaves.

lamb korma

Many people think of korma as a 'safe' dish to order because of its mild taste, but in India it's not only mildness that's important – a creamy texture is essential too. In this case it's created with a paste made from cashew nuts. The same method can be used to make korma dishes with other meat or poultry. You may like to serve the korma with yogurt and a sprinkling of garam masala.

SERVES 4–6

2.5cm (1 inch) piece fresh root ginger, peeled and chopped

4 garlic cloves, peeled

3 tablespoons vegetable oil

2.5cm (1 inch) piece cinnamon stick

3 cloves

2 bay leaves

3 cardamom pods, crushed

pinch of fennel seeds

2 onions, peeled and chopped

1 teaspoon ground coriander

1/4 teaspoon ground turmeric

1/2 teaspoon chilli powder

2 teaspoons tomato purée

500g (1lb 2oz) boneless lamb, cubed

pinch of ground black pepper

40g (1½oz) cashew nuts

1 tablespoon coriander leaves

handful of toasted cashew nuts, to serve

1   Using a mortar and pestle, grind the ginger and garlic together to make a fine paste; set aside. Heat the oil in a saucepan, karahi or wok. Add the cinnamon stick, cloves, bay leaves, cardamom, fennel seeds and onions and sauté for 5 minutes or until the onions are soft.

2   Add the ginger-garlic paste, then the ground coriander, turmeric, chilli powder and tomato purée. Mix well and cook over a low heat for 5 minutes, stirring occasionally. Stir in the lamb and black pepper and pour in 150ml (1/4 pint) water. Cover and simmer gently for 30 minutes or until the lamb is tender.

3   Meanwhile, using a mortar and pestle, grind the cashew nuts with a little water to make a smooth paste. When the lamb is cooked, add the cashew nut paste and stir well. Simmer for 3 minutes, then remove from the heat and serve scattered with coriander leaves and toasted cashew nuts.

lamb with coconut slivers

I first came across this dish in a restaurant in New Delhi, where I started my catering career. It was the most popular item on the menu by a long way. People are fascinated by the spicy flavour of this dish, and the stronger the better, if you can handle it. Beef can be used in place of the lamb, if you prefer.

SERVES 4–6

2.5cm (1 inch) piece fresh root ginger, peeled and sliced

3 garlic cloves, peeled and chopped

2.5cm (1 inch) piece cinnamon stick

2 bay leaves

3 cloves

20 curry leaves

5 tablespoons vegetable oil

2 onions, peeled and finely chopped

1 tablespoon ground coriander

1/2 teaspoon ground turmeric

1/2 teaspoon chilli powder

100g (3 1/2 oz) coconut, shaved into slivers

500g (1lb 2oz) boneless lamb, cubed

1/2 teaspoon mustard seeds

2 green chillies, slit lengthways

1   Using a small spice mill or mortar and pestle, grind the ginger, garlic, cinnamon stick, bay leaves, cloves and 10 curry leaves together. Set aside.

2   Heat 3 tablespoons oil in a large saucepan, karahi or wok. Add the onions and fry, stirring occasionally, for 5 minutes or until soft. Add the freshly ground spice mixture, the ground coriander, turmeric, chilli powder, coconut slivers and 400ml (14 fl oz) water. Bring the mixture to the boil, then add the lamb. Lower the heat and simmer gently for 30 minutes or until the lamb is well cooked.

3   Heat the remaining oil in a separate small frying pan. Add the mustard seeds and, when they start to pop, add the remaining 10 curry leaves and the chillies. Stir-fry for 1 minute, then add the contents of the pan to the cooked meat and continue cooking, stirring frequently, for about 10 minutes or until the lamb mixture is very dry. Serve hot, with naan or other Indian bread.

lamb and potato curry

Chef Madhu introduced me to this style of lamb curry. While working at a famous restaurant in Delhi, he used to make the dish frequently for India's former chief minister. Madhu recommends a hot Malabar paratha (page 155) to accompany it, but any bread will do. Substitute the lamb with beef, if you prefer.

SERVES 4–6

5 tablespoons vegetable oil

2.5cm (1 inch) piece fresh root ginger, peeled and chopped

4 garlic cloves, peeled and chopped

2 green chillies, chopped

15 curry leaves

2 onions, peeled and sliced

2 teaspoons ground coriander

1/2 teaspoon ground turmeric

1/2 teaspoon chilli powder

3 tomatoes, sliced

400g (14oz) boneless lamb, cubed

200g (7oz) baby new potatoes, scrubbed

1 teaspoon mustard seeds

1 Heat 4 tablespoons oil in a saucepan. Add the ginger, garlic, chillies and 5 curry leaves and sauté for 3 minutes or until the ginger and garlic are golden brown. Add the onions and cook, stirring frequently, for 10 minutes until lightly browned.

2 Stir in the ground coriander, turmeric and chilli powder, mix well, then add the tomatoes, lamb and 400ml (14fl oz) water. Bring to a simmer and cook over a low heat for 15 minutes.

3 Stir in the new potatoes and continue cooking for 15 minutes or until the lamb is cooked and the potatoes are tender.

4 Meanwhile, heat the remaining 1 tablespoon oil in a small frying pan. Add the mustard seeds and, when they start to pop, add the remaining 10 curry leaves and stir well. Pour the contents of the frying pan over the lamb mixture, stir briefly, then remove the pan from the heat and serve hot.

rogan josh

Almonds are a speciality of Kashmir and many parts of Northern India. They are most commonly used in sweet dishes, however, rogan josh, a richly flavoured lamb curry featuring ground almonds, is one exception. My friend Abdullah gave me this recipe. He is from Kashmir, where the dish is said to have originated. The combination of yogurt and almonds is unusual and I hope you like it.

SERVES 4

5 tablespoons vegetable oil
2 bay leaves
1 red onion, peeled and chopped
400g (14oz) boneless lamb, cubed
5 tablespoons ground almonds
sea salt

FOR THE SPICE PASTE:

500g (1lb 2oz) natural yogurt
2.5cm (1 inch) piece fresh root ginger,
  peeled and chopped
2 teaspoons garam masala
1 teaspoon chilli powder
1/2 teaspoon fennel seeds
large pinch of ground cardamom

1 To make the spice paste, place all the ingredients in a blender and process until smooth. Set aside.

2 Heat the oil in a large saucepan. Add the bay leaves and red onion and sauté over a medium heat for 2 minutes.

3 Add the lamb and stir-fry for 5 minutes or until the meat is evenly browned. Slowly add the spice paste, stirring constantly to help the meat absorb the essence of the paste. Reduce the heat to low, cover and cook gently for 30 minutes or until the lamb is tender.

4 Add the ground almonds and salt to taste. Serve hot with Malabar parathas (page 155).

stir-fried dry beef curry

In India, this spicy dish is known as *beef olathiathu* and is commonly served as a bar snack. It is very different from saucy curries, as the cooked beef cubes should be dry enough to pick up with the fingers. *Olathiathu* essentially means 'stir-fried' and, although our method is very different from the Chinese style you may be familiar with, it is an important technique to give the meat the correct dry, yet succulent, texture. Feel free to make this dish hotter and spicier if you want to. Serve it with appams (pages 158–9), and a moru curry (page 88–9) if you like.

SERVES 4-6

500g (1lb 2oz) silverside beef, cubed
1/2 teaspoon ground turmeric
1/2 teaspoon chilli powder
3 tablespoons vegetable oil
5 garlic cloves, peeled and chopped
1 large onion, peeled and sliced
1 1/2 teaspoons ground coriander
1 teaspoon ground black pepper
1 teaspoon garam masala
20 curry leaves
sea salt

1   Place the beef, turmeric and chilli powder in a large saucepan or casserole. Pour in 400ml (14fl oz) water and bring to a simmer, then cover and cook gently for 30 minutes or until the beef is tender. Add salt to taste, then remove the pan from the heat and set aside.

2   Shortly before the beef has finished simmering, heat the oil in a large frying pan, karahi or wok. Add the garlic and sauté until it is brown, then add the onion and cook, stirring occasionally, for 10 minutes or until golden. Sprinkle in the ground coriander and sauté for 2 minutes.

3   Drain the excess liquid from the cooked beef mixture, then transfer the meat to the pan of spicy onions. Add the black pepper, garam masala and curry leaves and cook, stirring, over a medium heat for 10 minutes until the mixture is very dry. Serve hot.

7 breads and rice

pooris

These light pooris are easy to make, look appetising and taste good. Poori masala is one of the best breakfast dishes you will find in any part of India. The combination of hot, puffy pooris served with freshly made potato masala is a regular item in railway canteens, and home kitchens. Pooris are also excellent with dry chicken and lamb dishes.

MAKES 6

200g (7oz) plain flour, plus extra to dust
1/2 tablespoon vegetable oil
vegetable oil, for deep-frying
sea salt

1   Place the flour in a large bowl with a generous pinch of salt. Gradually stir in the oil, then about 100ml (3½fl oz) water or just enough to make a smooth dough. Cover and set aside for 10 minutes.

2   Knead the dough on a lightly floured work surface for 2–3 minutes. Divide the dough into 6 equal portions, about the size of a golf ball. Roll each ball out as thinly as possible to make a neat round.

3   Heat the oil for deep-frying in a deep-fryer, wok or large, heavy-based saucepan to 180–190°C or until a cube of bread browns in 30 seconds. At the same time, place a cast-iron griddle or a large, heavy-based frying pan over a high heat to heat thoroughly.

4   Working one at a time, toast the circles of dough on the hot, unoiled griddle pan for 30 seconds on each side. Then, using a spatula or fish slice, transfer the poori to the hot oil and deep-fry for about 2 minutes, turning constantly, to help it puff up. Remove from the pan and drain on kitchen paper while you toast and deep-fry the remaining dough rounds. Serve immediately.

chapattis

The majority of Indian people eat chapattis at most meals, serving them with curries or even simply a pickle. They are the most popular of all Indian breads, and you will find them on Indian restaurant menus all over the world. The ease with which they are made is a key advantage and they will complement most of the savoury dishes in this book.

MAKES 8

400g (14oz) wholemeal flour, plus extra
  to dust
2 teaspoons vegetable oil
sea salt

1 Place the flour and a pinch of salt in a large bowl. Gradually stir in the oil, then mix in about 200ml (7fl oz) water to make a smooth dough.

2 Knead the dough on a lightly floured work surface for about 3 minutes, then divide the mixture into 8 equal portions, about the size of a golf ball. Working one at a time, roll out the balls of dough as thinly as possible, turning them frequently to make an even circle.

3 Heat a flat cast-iron griddle pan or large, heavy-based frying pan. When thoroughly hot, cook the chapattis in batches as necessary. Place on the griddle pan and toast for 1–2 minutes each side or until the dough is cooked and very lightly speckled, turning them frequently. Remove and keep warm while you cook the remaining chapattis. Serve immediately.

Malabar parathas

This rich-tasting South Indian flat bread is invariably well received the first time anyone tastes it, and it is an essential order for regular customers at our restaurants. The dough is rolled and coiled to make a flaky bread that pulls apart temptingly in mouthwatering layers, yet it is made from a simple combination of wholemeal flour and oil. Malabar paratha is an excellent accompaniment to Kerala's light vegetable curries.

MAKES 4

125g (4oz) wholemeal flour, plus extra
  to dust
2 tablespoons vegetable oil, plus extra
  for oiling

1 Place the flour in a large bowl. Gradually stir in the vegetable oil and about 150ml (¼ pint) water or just enough to make a soft dough. Knead the dough on a work surface for 3–4 minutes, then return to the bowl, cover and set aside to rest for 1 hour.

2 Divide the dough into 4 equal portions. Keeping the unused portions covered to prevent them drying out, take one piece of dough and roll it into a ball, then dust lightly with flour.

3 On a clean work surface or board, roll out the dough to a circle about 15 cm (6 inches) diameter and brush the top lightly with a thin layer of vegetable oil. Roll up the dough to make a long, thin cigar shape, then carefully place one end of the dough in the middle of your palm and wind the rest around and around to make a coil.

4 Flatten the coiled dough with the palms of your hands and dust with flour. Return it to the work surface and carefully roll it out into a 12cm (5 inch) circle. Cover and set aside while you repeat the process with the remaining balls of dough.

5 Place a flat cast-iron griddle pan over a medium-high heat for 8–10 minutes or until very hot. Place 1–2 parathas on it and sprinkle with a little oil. Cook, turning frequently, for about 2–3 minutes on each side or until golden and cooked. Keep warm while you cook the rest, then serve warm.

adipoli parathas

Our special seafood-flavoured bread is based on the popular Ceylonese tradition of flat, thin bread dough stuffed with a combination of spices and seafood masala. It has a wonderful rich flavour and crispy texture, and has been described as a complete meal in itself.

MAKES 8

225 g (8oz) wholemeal flour, plus extra to dust

4 tablespoons vegetable oil, plus extra to brush

FOR THE FILLING:

8 tablespoons vegetable oil

1/2 teaspoon mustard seeds

2.5cm (1 inch) piece fresh root ginger, peeled and grated

2 onions, peeled and finely chopped

1 green chilli, chopped

10 curry leaves

1/2 teaspoon ground turmeric

150g (5oz) raw prawns, peeled

2 eggs, beaten

sea salt

1 To make the dough, place the wholemeal flour in a large bowl. Gradually stir in the oil and about 150ml (1/4 pint) water to make a soft, pliable dough. Knead on a work surface for 3–4 minutes, then return to the bowl, cover and set aside for 1 hour.

2 To make the filling, heat the oil in a frying pan. Add the mustard seeds and, when they start to pop, add the ginger, onions, chilli and curry leaves. Cook over a medium-low heat for 5 minutes, stirring occasionally, until the onions are soft. Add the turmeric and a little salt and sauté for 1 minute. Add the prawns and cook for 7–10 minutes, stirring occasionally, until they have turned pink and are cooked. Remove the frying pan from the heat and set aside.

3 Divide the dough into 8 equal portions. Place one piece in the palm of your hands and roll it into a smooth ball. Lightly dust with flour, then place it on a board and roll out as thinly as possible, to make a paper-thin circle, about 22cm (8 1/2 inches) in diameter.

4 Heat a flat cast-iron griddle or large, heavy-based frying pan. Brush with oil and, when hot, add a circle of dough. Stir the eggs into the prawn mixture, then spread 3 tablespoons of this filling on top of the dough on the griddle pan. Cook over a medium heat for 5 minutes or until browned underneath.

5 Lower the heat, then carefully turn the paratha over with a spatula and cook for a further 5 minutes or until the prawn mixture is well stuck to the paratha. Turn it over again and transfer the paratha to a board. Roll the paratha into a cylinder shape to enclose the prawn mixture. Repeat with the remaining dough and filling. Cut each paratha into 2 or 3 pieces before serving.

appams

These soft, spongy pancakes, made from fermented white rice, are a typical dish of the Keralan Christian community. They are particularly popular at Easter, when they are served with lamb stew and other delicacies.

Appams have a naturally sweet flavour that is unique. They are also relatively easy to make. In the restaurants we like to be a little flamboyant, so we make them to order in front of customers, using a special curved pan called a chatti that looks like a small cast-iron wok. However, they also look inviting cooked simply on a flat griddle or frying pan at home.

In Kerala we tend to eat appams with mildly flavoured stews, but they can also provide a good contrast to spicier dishes. Alternatively, you can serve them simply as a snack, with a good fresh chutney. However, my favourite way to eat appams is drizzled with a few tablespoons of coconut milk and sprinkled with little sugar for breakfast.

▲ **onion masala appams**
Make the batter as for basic appams. Heat 2 tbsp oil in a pan, add ½ tsp mustard seeds and, as they start to pop, add 10 curry leaves and 1 chopped red onion and cook for 5 minutes. Add 1 sliced green chilli and cook for a further 2 minutes. Cook the pancakes as for basic appams, but after 2 minutes' cooking, gently spread 1 tbsp of the onion mixture on top. Carefully turn the pancake over and cook for about 3 minutes until the onion is golden and embedded in batter. Repeat to make 4–6 appams.

▼ basic appams

Wash 250g (9oz) basmati rice, then soak in fresh cold water to cover for 1 hour. Drain, reserving 225ml (7½fl oz) water. Put the rice and reserved water in a blender and process to a batter. Add 125g (4oz) freshly grated coconut and blend until fine; set aside. In a bowl, dissolve 1 tsp sugar in 5 tsp warm water, then add 1 tsp fast-action dried yeast; cover and set aside. Put 75g (3oz) semolina in a pan with 100ml (3½fl oz)

egg appams

Make the batter as for basic appams. Heat an oiled griddle or non-stick frying pan. Add a ladleful of batter and spread thinly to make a large pancake. Cover and cook for 2 minutes, then remove lid and crack an egg into the middle of the appam. Re-cover and cook for further 2–3 minutes or until the base is golden and crisp and the egg is lightly cooked. Transfer to a plate and serve. You will need 4–6 eggs to use all the batter.

water and cook for 15 minutes or until thick. Transfer to a bowl, add the rice batter and yeast mix, stir well and cover with a damp cloth. Set aside for 4 hours or until the batter is bubbly and doubled in volume. Stir in 1 tsp salt, carefully to avoid knocking air out of the batter. Heat an oiled griddle pan or non-stick frying pan. Add a ladleful of batter and spread out thinly to make a large pancake. Cover and cook for 2 minutes on one side only, so the top remains moist; carefully remove. Repeat to make 4–6 appams.

▲ sweet appams

Make the batter as for basic appams. Just before cooking, mix 4 tbsp thin honey with 4 tbsp palm sugar, grated if necessary (or just use 6 tbsp honey). Heat an oiled griddle pan or non-stick frying pan. Add a ladleful of batter and spread out thinly to make a large pancake. Cover and cook for 2 minutes on one side only, so the top remains moist. Repeat to make 4–6 appams. Serve hot, drizzled with the honey mixture and sprinkled with grated coconut if desired.

vermicelli and rice

The first time I ate this rice and noodle dish in a Brahmin home, I thought it was delicious. Adding tempered spices gives a wonderful flavour and makes it rather like a complete dish that could be eaten without curries alongside. Otherwise, it makes a good alternative to plain rice.

SERVES 4

3 tablespoons ghee
100g (3½oz) vermicelli
2 tablespoons vegetable oil
½ teaspoon mustard seeds
1 teaspoon urad dal
10 curry leaves
25g (1oz) cashew nuts

2 green chillies, finely chopped
2.5cm (1 inch) piece fresh root ginger,
  peeled and grated
50g (2oz) freshly grated coconut
100g (3½oz) white rice, cooked
sea salt
2 tablespoons chopped coriander, plus
  a few whole leaves, to serve

1 Heat the ghee in a large frying pan over a medium heat. When hot, add the vermicelli and stir-fry for 5–6 minutes or until golden. Remove with a slotted spoon and set aside to drain on kitchen paper.

2 Heat the oil in another frying pan. Add the mustard seeds, urad dal, curry leaves and cashew nuts and fry for 1–2 minutes or until the nuts and urad dal turn brown. Add the chillies, ginger and a little salt, then pour in 400ml (14fl oz) water and bring to the boil. Lower the heat, add the vermicelli and simmer for 3–4 minutes until thoroughly blended with the spices.

3 Add the grated coconut and cooked rice. Carefully mix with the vermicelli and allow to warm through briefly. Transfer to a serving bowl, scatter with coriander and serve.

boiled rice

Rice is a key part of any Indian meal. In Kerala I was used to eating full-flavoured homegrown red rice, but in North India basmati rice is very popular because of its pure white colour, clean flavour and exotic fragrance. Basmati is now widely available here and easy to cook.

SERVES 4

200g (7oz) white basmati or other
  long-grain white rice
sea salt

1 Wash the rice in plenty of cold water, then drain and place in a large, heavy-based saucepan. Add 750ml (1¼ pints) fresh water and a little salt and stir well. Place the saucepan over a high heat and bring to the boil. Lower the heat slightly and simmer for 20 minutes or until the rice is cooked. Drain thoroughly and serve hot.

vegetable rice

This is a variation of a colourful rice dish typically served with an array of dishes at special functions in India. Personally, I find it is delicious eaten on its own with a simple raita. The use of ghee gives it a special richness.

SERVES 4–6

2 green chillies

2.5cm (1 inch) piece fresh root ginger, peeled and chopped

2 garlic cloves, peeled

400g (14oz) white basmati rice

4 tablespoons vegetable oil

1/2 teaspoon cumin seeds

1 cinnamon stick

5 cardamom pods

10 curry leaves

2 onions, peeled and finely chopped

1/2 teaspoon ground turmeric

1 teaspoon chilli powder

3 tomatoes, chopped

100g (3 1/2 oz) potato, peeled and diced

100g (3 1/2 oz) cauliflower florets

75g (3oz) peas

2 tablespoons ghee

sea salt

2 tablespoons chopped coriander leaves, to serve

1 Using a small spice mill or mortar and pestle, grind the chillies, ginger and garlic together to make a fine paste. Set aside. Wash the rice in plenty of cold water and set aside to drain thoroughly.

2 Heat the oil in a large saucepan. Add the cumin seeds, cinnamon, cardamom pods and curry leaves and sauté for 1 minute, then add the onions and cook over a medium heat for 5 minutes, stirring occasionally. Add the fresh chilli paste and cook for a further 5 minutes or until the onions are golden. Add the turmeric, chilli powder, tomatoes and a little salt, and cook for 1 minute, stirring occasionally.

3 Add the rice, potato, cauliflower, peas and ghee and fry for 2 minutes. Pour in enough hot water to cover and give it a stir. Bring to the boil, then lower the heat and simmer for 20 minutes or until the rice and vegetables are cooked. Transfer to a serving dish and scatter with chopped coriander to serve.

cashew and lemon rice

With its fresh citrus flavour and the fragrance of curry leaves, this lemon rice has become the most popular of the rice specialities served in our restaurants. In Brahmin homes lemon rice is considered a special occasion dish. Adding cashew nuts, which are prolific in Kerala, makes the dish taste much richer, and chana dal adds its own nutty flavour. In my view, all you need to make it a complete meal is a yogurt curry (see pages 88–9) and a delicious thoran (see pages 42–3).
Illustrated on previous page

SERVES 4
200g (7oz) white long-grain or basmati rice
1/2 teaspoon ground turmeric
juice of 1/2 lemon
2 tablespoons vegetable oil
1 teaspoon mustard seeds
2 dried red chillies
1 teaspoon chana dal or urad dal
3–5 curry leaves, plus extra to garnish
50g (2oz) cashew nuts
sea salt

1   Wash the rice in plenty of cold water, then drain and place in a large, heavy-based saucepan. Add 750ml (1 1/4 pints) water, the turmeric and a little salt. Stir well and bring to the boil over a high heat. Lower the heat slightly and simmer for 20 minutes or until the rice is cooked. Drain thoroughly and return to the saucepan. Stir in the lemon juice and set aside in a warm place.

2   Heat the oil in a small frying pan. Add the mustard seeds and, when they start to pop, add the dried red chillies, chana dal, curry leaves and cashew nuts. Stir-fry for 2–3 minutes or until the chana dal and cashew nuts are lightly browned, then pour the contents of the frying pan over the lemon rice.

3   Transfer the rice to a large serving dish, garnish with a few extra curry leaves and serve immediately.

Muslim-style rice with ghee

Biryani and similar richly flavoured rice dishes are specialities of India's Muslim communities, but recipes vary widely around the subcontinent. In Kerala, the Malabar region is particularly known for its Islamic cooking and this simple, yet delicious rice preparation is served with spicy meat dishes. I have found it excellent with mild curries too. Ghee is normally associated with special rice preparations, but here its flavour is integral to the success of the dish.

SERVES 4–5

250g (9oz) basmati rice
6 tablespoons ghee
50g (2oz) cashew nuts
1 tablespoon raisins
5 cardamom pods, lightly crushed
1 large onion, peeled and chopped
sea salt

1   Wash the basmati rice thoroughly in plenty of cold water, then drain and set aside in a sieve to drain thoroughly.

2   Heat the ghee in a large saucepan. Add the cashew nuts, raisins and cardamom pods and fry for 2–3 minutes until the cashews turn golden. Add the onion and cook, stirring frequently, for 5 minutes or until it is soft and lightly golden.

3   Stir in the drained rice and stir-fry for 5 minutes or until the rice grains are translucent. Add 1 litre (1¾ pints) water and a little salt. Bring to the boil, then lower the heat, cover the saucepan and cook gently for 20 minutes or until the rice is tender and all the water has been absorbed. Serve hot.

8 desserts and drinks

Rasa fruit salad

We used to eat a lot of different fruits in our village, but fruit salad wasn't something I tried until I visited restaurants in the city. This one is a fantastic blend of various fruits and juices, and the perfect finish to a lovely meal.

SERVES 4–6
1 small pineapple
1 large wedge of watermelon
100g (3¹/₂oz) seedless green grapes, halved
100g (3¹/₂oz) seedless red grapes, halved
2 oranges
1 seedless guava or mango
100ml (3¹/₂fl oz) mango juice
100ml (3¹/₂fl oz) passion fruit juice
5 tablespoons lime juice
20g (³/₄oz) mint leaves, shredded

1 Cut away the skin from the pineapple, remove the 'eyes', then quarter, core and cut the flesh into chunks. Place the pineapple in a large salad bowl. Remove the skin and seeds from the watermelon, then cut into chunks. Add to the pineapple together with the grapes.

2 Peel the oranges, removing all white pith, then cut out the segments and add to the prepared fruit. Peel and chop the guava or mango and add to the bowl.

3 Pour the mango and passion fruit juices over the fruits and toss to mix. Add the lime juice, stir gently and scatter over the chopped mint leaves. Serve in individual dishes, with a scoop of coconut or vanilla ice cream if you like.

carrot pudding

In India we make a number of desserts from carrots, including halwa which is from the North. In South India, milky puddings called *payasam* are more popular. These are prepared in various ways, using different fruits, grains and nuts. This pudding is a favourite at my sister's home.

SERVES 4

1.2 litres (2 pints) milk
pinch of powdered saffron
250g (9oz) carrots, peeled
3 tablespoons ghee
150g (5oz) caster sugar

50g (2oz) pistachio nuts, skinned
25g (1oz) blanched almonds, chopped
1 teaspoon ground cardamom
extra pistachio nuts and almonds, to serve
  (optional)

1 Pour 3 tablespoons of the milk into a small bowl, add the saffron and set aside to infuse for 5–10 minutes until the milk is orange in colour. Slowly bring the remaining milk to the boil in a large saucepan, then simmer over a medium heat for 10 minutes. Lower the heat and continue to simmer, stirring, for 20 minutes.

2 Meanwhile, grate the carrots. Heat the ghee in a frying pan. Add the grated carrots and gently fry for 5 minutes or until lightly golden.

3 Tip the carrots into a blender, add the sugar and 4–5 tablespoons of the hot milk and process to a coarse paste. Add this to the simmering milk and stir well. Continue cooking over a low heat for a further 10 minutes.

4 Meanwhile, roughly grind the pistachios using a small spice mill or mortar and pestle. Add to the simmering carrot mixture with the chopped almonds, then mix in the saffron milk and cardamom. Simmer for a few more minutes, then take off the heat. Serve hot or cold, topped with shredded almonds and pistachio nuts if you like.

strawberry and banana pudding

This easy dessert was devised during one of my evening cookery classes. It was so successful it's now a regular item on our restaurant menus too. You can use any ripe fruit, but I love the combination of banana and strawberries.
Illustrated on previous page

SERVES 4
5 tablespoons ghee
50g (2oz) cashew nuts
50g (2oz) raisins
150g (5oz) palm sugar
400ml (14fl oz) coconut milk
pinch of ground cardamom
250g (9oz) strawberries, sliced
2 bananas, peeled and chopped

1 Heat 3 tablespoons ghee in a frying pan. Add the cashew nuts and fry for 2–3 minutes or until golden, adding the raisins after 1–2 minutes so that they plump up slightly. Remove the pan from the heat and set aside.

2 Put the palm sugar in a saucepan with 250ml (8fl oz) water and place over a low heat. Stir until the sugar dissolves, then increase the heat and simmer for 5 minutes. Add 2 tablespoons ghee and continue cooking for a further 5 minutes or until the sauce thickens.

3 Lower the heat, add the coconut milk and simmer gently, stirring occasionally, for 10 minutes. Stir in the cardamom, then add the toasted cashew nuts and raisins. Remove the pan from the heat. Gently stir the strawberries and bananas into the sauce and set aside to cool before serving.

vermicelli pudding

This dessert is very popular in South India, especially among Tamil people. It is often presented as part of a thali meal in restaurants specialising in Tamil cuisine, which can be found all over India. It is also made at home for special occasions.

SERVES 4

200g (7oz) vermicelli
6 tablespoons ghee
50g (2oz) cashew nuts
50g (2oz) raisins
1.2 litres (2 pints) milk
150g (5oz) caster sugar
pinch of powdered saffron

1 Break up the vermicelli into short pieces, about 3cm (1¼ inches) long, and set aside.

2 Heat the ghee in a large frying pan. Add the cashew nuts and gently fry for 2–3 minutes or until golden. Remove from the frying pan using a slotted spoon and set aside to drain on kitchen paper.

3 Add the raisins to the frying pan and fry, stirring, for 1 minute or until they are plump and toasted. Transfer them to the kitchen paper with a slotted spoon. Add the vermicelli to the frying pan and cook for 5 minutes or until it turns brown.

4 Bring the milk to the boil in a large, heavy-based saucepan over a medium heat. Simmer, stirring constantly, for 20 minutes or until the milk has reduced in volume by half. Lower the heat, then add the vermicelli and cook, stirring constantly, for 15 minutes.

5 Add the sugar, cashew nuts, raisins and saffron. Simmer, stirring, for 5 minutes or until thoroughly blended. Serve the vermicelli pudding hot.

panchamritham

Panchamritham is a traditional dessert associated with the Palani temple in Tamil Nadu in South India. I once visited this temple with my father, who used to make regular pilgrimages there, and was amazed to see a street full of shops making panchamritham. There was no shortage of buyers. This dessert is simple to make and has a good clean taste of honey and fruits. If plantain is unobtainable, simply use two bananas rather than one.

SERVES 4
1 banana
1 plantain
1 mango
3 tablespoons ghee
50g (2oz) fresh dates, halved and stoned
50g (2oz) raisins
50g (2oz) granulated sugar
3 tablespoons thin honey
pinch of ground cardamom

1   Peel and roughly chop the banana and plantain. Halve the mango, cut the flesh away from the stone, then cut into cubes and set aside.

2   Heat the ghee in a large frying pan. Add the banana, plantain, dates, raisins and sugar and fry gently for 5 minutes or until the mixtures browns slightly and the fruits are well blended with the ghee.

3   Remove the pan from the heat, add the honey, mango and ground cardamom and mix well. Set aside to cool, then chill in the refrigerator until ready to serve.

mango halwa

Last year we held a mango festival and created many dishes using mangoes brought over from India, including this one. Halwa originates from the Muslim community and is normally time-consuming to make, but this is a simplified version. It has a delicious flavour and soft texture.

SERVES 4–6

4 tablespoons ghee
50g (2oz) freshly grated coconut
50g (2oz) semolina
450g (1lb) well drained, canned mango

150g (5oz) caster sugar, plus extra to sprinkle
200g (7oz) fresh mango flesh (about 1 large
  mango), diced and well drained
1 teaspoon ground cardamom
chopped pistachio nuts, to serve

1 Heat 1 tablespoon ghee in a large frying pan. Add the coconut and fry for 3 minutes or until golden. Remove with a slotted spoon and set aside to drain on kitchen paper. Add the semolina to the frying pan and cook over a low heat for 5 minutes or until golden. Remove from the pan and set aside. Purée the canned mango pieces in a blender or food processor to give 450g (1lb) pulp.

2 Put the sugar and 600ml (1 pint) water in a large, heavy-based saucepan. Heat slowly, stirring until the sugar dissolves, then increase the heat and bring to the boil. Add the mango pulp and 2 tablespoons ghee. Turn the heat down to medium and cook for 35 minutes until well reduced, stirring frequently to prevent the mixture sticking to the pan.

3 Add the remaining 1 tablespoon of ghee and cook for a further 15 minutes, stirring frequently, until the mixture is very thick. Sprinkle in the toasted semolina and cook for a further 15 minutes or until the mixture is smooth and comes away easily from the sides of the pan.

4 Add the fresh mango, toasted coconut and cardamom. Stir well, then pour the mixture into an oiled baking tin, about 25x20cm (10x8 inches). Leave to cool, then chill overnight until set. Cut into pieces and serve cold or at room temperature, sprinkled with pistachios and a little extra sugar.

kulfi

Kulfi, India's famously rich ice cream, is a regular feature on every Indian restaurant menu in Britain, but back home it is a cooling streetfood. Kulfi men on bicycles sell the ices to children and grown-ups alike. Everyone relishes the amazing taste, especially in summertime. The best fruit flavours change according to what is in season, but other varieties based on nuts and spices are made all year round.

Kulfi was first prepared for the grand Moguls, whose cuisine is Persian-influenced. In those days, clay pots were used as moulds, but today lidded metal cones are more common. You can use any suitable freezerproof container, either individual moulds about 175ml (6fl oz) capacity, or a large container – slicing the ice cream to serve. Remember to soften kulfi at room temperature for 5 minutes before serving.

These recipes are based on my own style of kulfi making. Each makes 8–10 servings.

▲ mango kulfi

Purée a drained 410g can mango pieces in a blender until smooth. Measure 150ml (¼ pint) mango purée and stir in a pinch of ground cardamom. Fold into the kulfi base with 150ml (¼ pint) lightly whipped double cream. Freeze in a suitable container for 1 hour. Remove, whisk well, then freeze for another 1 hour. Repeat whisking and freezing twice more then freeze, in individual moulds if liked, for 4–5 hours or overnight. Soften at room temperature for 5 minutes to serve.

for the kulfi base

Bring 4 litres (7 pints) milk to the boil in a heavy-based pan. Lower the heat slightly and simmer for 45 minutes or until thickened and reduced by half. Cool slightly. In a bowl, mix 1 tbsp rice flour with 2 tbsp of the milk until smooth. Pour into the pan and cook for 15 minutes, stirring, until the milk has reduced to the consistency of a pouring sauce. Add 175g (6oz) caster sugar and stir until dissolved. Cool completely.

for a saffron kulfi base

Follow the method for the standard kulfi base, adding 1 tsp saffron threads to the reduced milk when you stir in the sugar.

almond kulfi

Fold 25g (1oz) ground almonds, 25g (1oz) sliced almonds, a few drops of almond extract and 150ml (¼ pint) lightly whipped double cream into the cooled kulfi base. Freeze in a suitable container for 1 hour, then remove and whisk well. Return to the freezer for 1 hour. Repeat the whisking and freezing process twice more, then freeze, in individual moulds if liked, for 4–5 hours or overnight. Soften the kulfi at room temperature for 5 minutes before serving.

▲ pistachio kulfi

Add 50g (2oz) crushed pistachio nuts and a few drops of rose water to the cooled kulfi base, mix well, then fold in 150ml (¼ pint) lightly whipped double cream. Freeze in a suitable container for 1 hour, then remove and whisk thoroughly. Return to the freezer for 1 hour. Repeat the whisking and freezing process twice more, then freeze, in individual moulds if liked, for 4–5 hours or overnight. Soften the kulfi at room temperature for 5 minutes to serve.

Keralan lassi

In Kerala, this is the drink you will be offered on a hot afternoon. The fresh taste of spices with clean, thin homemade yogurt is wonderfully refreshing and the best relief for hardworking farmers during their lunchbreak. Recently it has become the fashion to serve this drink in restaurants, where it has become known as Keralan lassi because of its spicy flavour.

SERVES 3–4

300g (11oz) yogurt
2.5cm (1 inch) piece fresh root ginger,
 peeled and sliced
2–3 shallots, peeled and sliced
2 green chillies, chopped
few curry leaves
pinch of cumin seeds
pinch of ground cumin
sea salt

1 Place the yogurt, ginger, shallots, chopped chillies, curry leaves and a little salt in a blender. Add 300ml (½ pint) water and process until smooth and thoroughly blended. Pour into a jug and chill until ready to serve.

2 Briefly toast the cumin seeds in a dry frying pan over a medium heat until fragrant, then remove from the heat.

3 When ready to serve, place some crushed ice in each glass, pour in the lassi and sprinkle with the ground cumin and toasted cumin seeds.

banana lassi

This is one of my favourite drinks and it was my regular order at the refreshment kiosk during my school years. The thought of flavourful bananas blended with cold yogurt, our local sugar and a touch of cardamom still makes my mouth water.

SERVES 2–4

250g (9oz) natural yogurt
200g (7oz) banana, cubed
125ml (4fl oz) milk
4 teaspoons sugar
1/2 teaspoon ground cardamom
1 tablespoon pistachio nuts, crushed

1 Place the yogurt, banana, milk and sugar in a blender and blend until very smooth. Stir in the ground cardamom.

2 Place some crushed ice in a serving jug or individual glasses and pour the lassi over. Sprinkle with the crushed pistachio nuts and serve.

almond milk shake

I am very partial to this Indian-style milk shake. It's a lovely combination of flavours and is very tasty served chilled.

SERVES 4

2 tablespoons blanched almonds
2 tablespoons pistachio nuts
450ml (3/4 pint) milk
2 tablespoons brown sugar
1/2 teaspoon ground cardamom

1 Place the almonds and pistachio nuts in a blender, add 100ml (3½fl oz) water and work to a coarse paste. Add the milk and brown sugar and process for a further 2 minutes or until smooth and well blended.

2 Divide the milk shake among 4 serving glasses. Add some crushed ice, then sprinkle with ground cardamom and serve immediately.

tangy carrot juice

I have fond memories of New Delhi juice bars, which offer the best selection I have ever seen. People in North India consume a lot of different fresh juices and I am fascinated by their clever use of spices to make the drinks more interesting. My favourite additions to carrot juice are fresh mint and ginger.

SERVES 4

500g (1lb 2oz) carrots, peeled
2.5cm (1 inch) piece fresh root ginger,
  peeled and chopped
1 tablespoon mint leaves
2 tablespoons lime juice
sea salt

1 Cut the carrots into chunks, then push them through a juice extractor with the chopped ginger and mint leaves. Transfer the carrot juice to a jug, add sea salt to taste and the lime juice. Chill in the refrigerator before serving.

cardamom tea

Spiced milky tea is hugely popular in India and can be made with either complex spice blends or simple ones. This version is made using green cardamom pods, which have a sweet lemony flavour, plus fresh ginger. For authenticity, use Assam tea, which is a full-bodied style from North-east India.

SERVES 4

275ml (9fl oz) milk
2 tablespoons Assam tea leaves
2.5cm (1 inch) piece fresh root ginger,
  peeled and grated
5 green cardamom pods
sugar, to taste

1 Pour the milk into a small saucepan, add 275ml (9fl oz) water and bring to the boil. Lower the heat slightly and add the tea leaves, ginger, cardamom and sugar to taste. Simmer gently for 5 minutes, stirring occasionally to ensure that the ingredients are well mixed.

2 Remove the pan from the heat and discard the cardamom pods. Pour the cardamom tea into cups and serve immediately.

watermelon and lime juice

Watermelons are readily available today and when summer temperatures are high, there is nothing better than this superb, refreshing juice. I hope you like it as much as I do.

SERVES 4

¹/₂ watermelon
2 tablespoons lime juice
1–2 tablespoons sugar, to taste (optional)
4 thin lime slices

1   Cut away the rind from the watermelon and remove the seeds with a teaspoon. Cut the flesh into manageable pieces. Push the watermelon flesh through a juice extractor. Alternatively, you can purée the watermelon in a blender, then sieve the juice.

2   Transfer the watermelon juice to a jug and add the lime juice. Taste and sweeten with a little sugar, if required, mixing well. Chill the juice in the refrigerator until ready to serve.

3   To serve, pour the chilled watermelon juice into 4 serving glasses. Add some crushed ice and a lime slice to each glass.

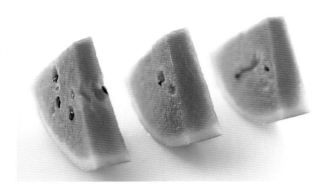

index